WILD
KITCHENS

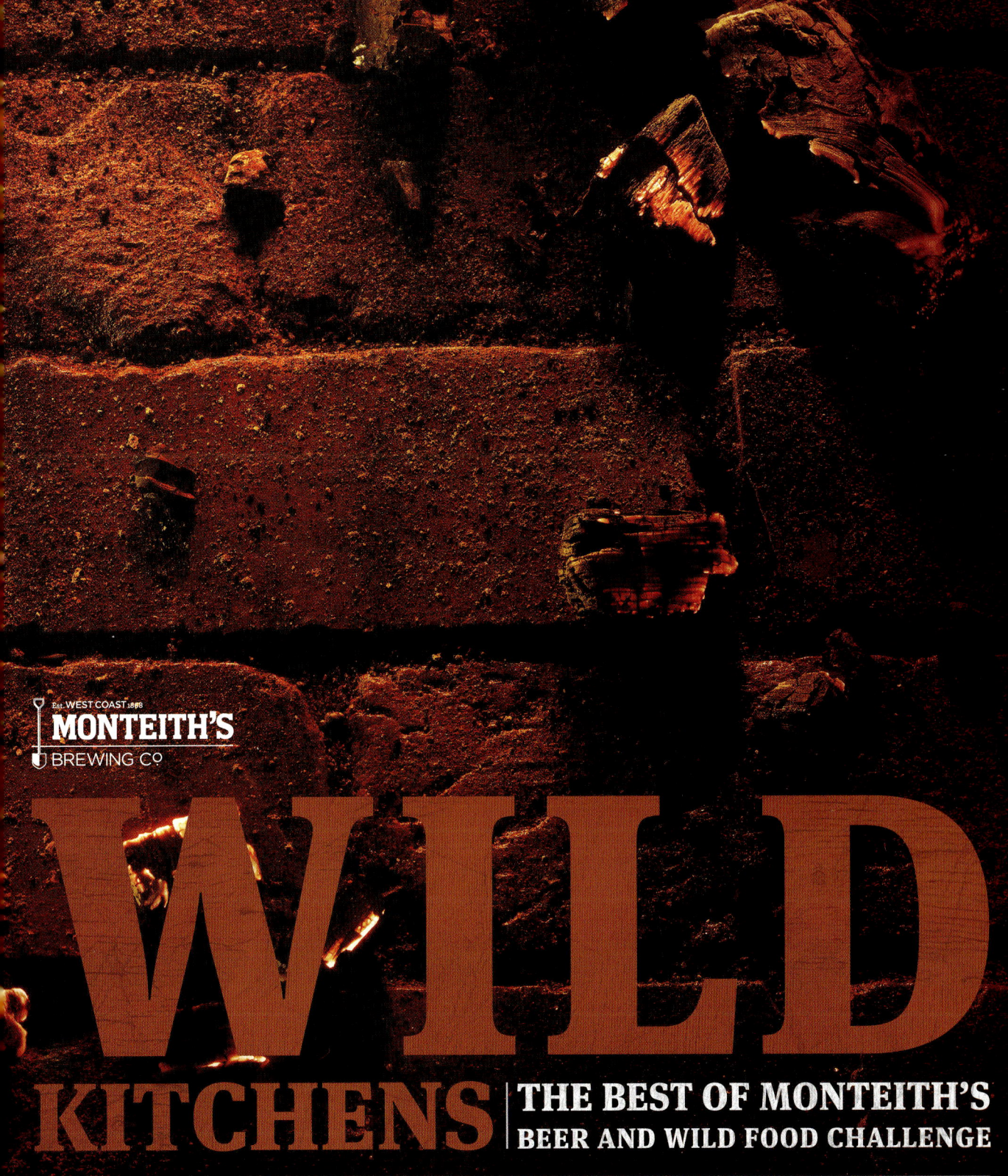

MONTEITH'S
Est. WEST COAST 1868
BREWING C°

WILD
KITCHENS | THE BEST OF MONTEITH'S
BEER AND WILD FOOD CHALLENGE

KERRY R. TYACK

HarperCollins*Publishers*

HarperCollins*Publishers*

First published in 2012
by HarperCollins*Publishers (New Zealand) Limited*
PO Box 1, Shortland Street, Auckland 1140

Copyright © Kerry R. Tyack 2012

HarperCollins*Publishers*
31 View Road, Glenfield, Auckland 0627, New Zealand
Level 13, 201 Elizabeth Street, Sydney, NSW 2000, Australia
A 53, Sector 57, Noida, UP, India
77–85 Fulham Palace Road, London, W6 8JB, United Kingdom
2 Bloor Street East, 20th floor, Toronto, Ontario M4W 1A8, Canada
10 East 53rd Street, New York, NY 10022, USA

National Library of New Zealand Cataloguing-in-Publication Data

Tyack, Kerry.
Monteith's wild kitchens : the best of Monteith's Beer and Wild
Food Challenge / Kerry R. Tyack.
ISBN 978-1-86950-991-0
1. Cooking (Wild foods)—New Zealand. I. Monteith's Brewing Co.
II. Monteith's Beer and Wild Food Challenge. III. Title.
641.690993—dc 23

ISBN: 978 186950 991 0

Cover and internal design by Kate Barraclough
Food photography by Devin Hart, The Vertical Line
Images courtesy of DB Breweries Ltd, unless otherwise stated. Bottle images by
Simon Harper; scenic images by Blackbox Photography
Food preparation by Alan Brown
Food styling by Kerry R. Tyack
Publisher: Vicki Marsdon

Cover recipe: Raukumara Red (page 58)
Back cover recipes, top to bottom: Boar Burger (page 50); A Deering Roulade (page 145);
Venison, Sweetie? (page 113)

Colour reproduction by Graphic Print Group, South Australia
Printed in China by RR Donnelley

drinkresponsibly.co.nz™

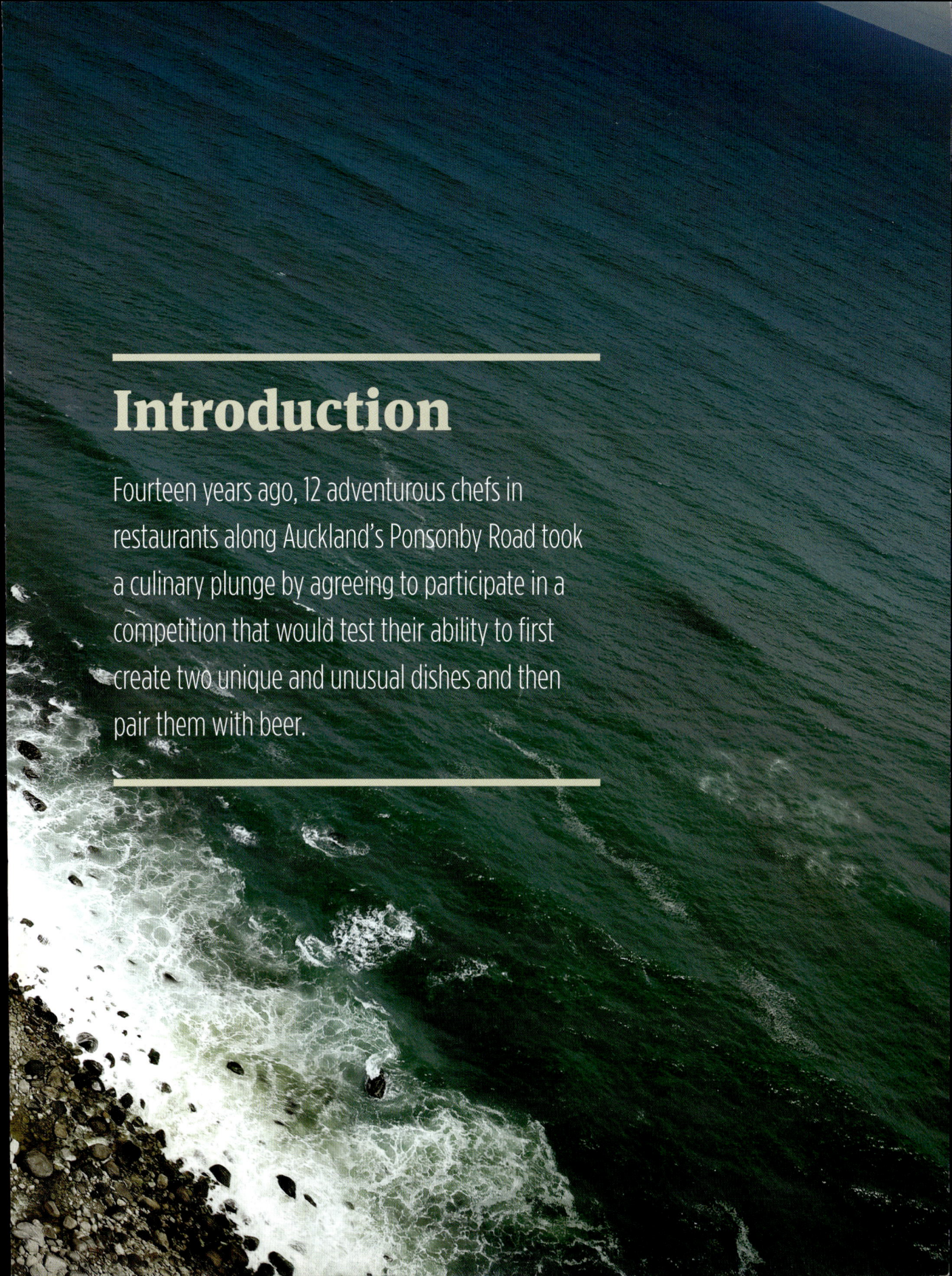

Introduction

Fourteen years ago, 12 adventurous chefs in restaurants along Auckland's Ponsonby Road took a culinary plunge by agreeing to participate in a competition that would test their ability to first create two unique and unusual dishes and then pair them with beer.

SMOOTH MALT AND
CRISP HOPS WITH
A SUBTLE BERRY-
FRUIT AROMA

FILE UNDER: BRITISH PUB BEERS

As with so many things in the kitchen, there was an extra catch; in this case, two catches. The first was that the significant ingredient in their creations had to be something from the wild waters, mountains or forests of New Zealand. The second was that the successful suitors to their dishes, the beers, had to be selected from those produced from a small West Coast brewery then unknown by most — Monteith's.

It was a challenge in the truest sense of the word. Happily, these chefs were up for it. That first Monteith's Wild Food Challenge created a unique set of benchmarks that would become the basis for New Zealand's longest-running competition for local restaurants; an event that with its unusual criteria remains unique in the world.

Nothing exercises the imagination of chefs more than the challenges provided by a cooking competition. The bar is raised when the challenge requires chefs to extend their levels of creativity to include a matching beverage.

> **I was convinced that a competition that simultaneously promoted creativity, involved the building of better communication between those who prepared the food and those who served it, and focused on good beer would appeal to chefs and restaurant operators.**

In the early 1990s, industry and consumer magazines in New Zealand and abroad were featuring increasing numbers of articles about what creative chefs and restaurant owners elsewhere in the world were doing to build custom. I was intrigued by the growing number of beer dinners on offer as a means of adding something new and exciting to the dining-out experience. A subsequent trip to the United States in the mid-1990s, where I visited a famous Poughkeepsie (New York State) restaurant well known for matching its food with local craft brews, convinced me that a similar thing would be possible in New Zealand. After all, it's not just the Americans making good beer, and it's not only on the sports field that Kiwis are competitive.

I was convinced that a competition that simultaneously promoted creativity, involved the building of better comm-unication between those who prepared the food and those who served it, and focused on good beer would appeal to chefs and restaurant operators.

A competition template already existed, which I had been involved in for a number of years, that had proved beyond all doubt that our chefs loved to test their skills against each other, especially when there was plenty of room for creativity. All we had to do was convince everyone that beer could legitimately be part of the contest.

Funding was the next issue and so I mapped out a proposal and sent it off to two major Auckland breweries. Within a week the public relations manager at DB Breweries, Sharon Buckland, called me and invited me in for a chat.

A few days later she called to say that Vaughan Smidt, the brand manager of Monteith's Brewing Company, a small sub-brand within the DB stable, was showing interest. At the time, Monteith's, well known on the West Coast of the South Island but hardly recognized beyond, was looking for a vehicle to promote itself in Auckland, and my challenge proposal, with its strong connection between beer and food, held significant possibilities.

> **In 2006, 163 restaurants in eight cities participated, which involved a panel of more than 90 judges over a three-week period.**

The first meeting with the amiable Vaughan focused on two possible hurdles. The current customer base for Monteith's in Auckland consisted of a few restaurants in the inner-city suburb of Ponsonby. These smallish owner-operated eateries tended to serve hot and hearty rather than haute cuisine. 'No problem,' I said, sensing my idea was striking the right chord. 'Let's build on the West Coast's reputation for being a bit wet and wild and incorporate a wild food component into the competition rules.'

Vaughan's second concern was the budget. There was simply not enough money in the Monteith's kitty for promoting it on a national scale.

'No problem,' said the ever-helpful Sharon Buckland. 'We'll keep it small and local to begin with and be prepared to expand if it's successful.' And so the Monteith's Wild Food Challenge was born.

Over the next few weeks we targeted around 20 restaurants in Auckland's Ponsonby and Jervois roads dining precinct, approaching them with an invitation to not only create two unique dishes using non-farmed produce but also to match each with a different beer from the Monteith's stable.

The initial interest was unexpectedly cautious and there was fear my project would fall over. I got on the phone and began calling those chefs I knew to encourage them to enter. By the time the first Challenge kicked off in the winter of 1998 we had 12 entrants.

Just nine years later in 2006, 163 restaurants in eight cities

participated, which involved a panel of more than 90 judges over a three-week period.

Although the first two years involved only the participating restaurants on Ponsonby and Jervois roads, the desire from chefs and restaurant operators around Auckland to be part of the competition meant that we expanded the Challenge catchment area to include Karangahape Road.

In subsequent years the competition extended out to Christchurch, Wellington and Dunedin, and then Hamilton and Tauranga. Queenstown came later in 2007, the tenth year, and Coromandel/Bay of Plenty and Nelson/Marlborough regions were included for the first time. However, it was some time before the magnificent West Coast, home to Monteith's, joined in. Initially there were issues around timing, plus the fact that the few restaurants in the region were spread over an enormous area.

Over the years the rules of the Challenge have frequently been tweaked. Interestingly, in this its fifteenth year, the rules are closer than ever to those established in the early days. An initial judging round using the skills of a team of expert regional judges has been reintroduced, thus satisfying the participants' desire for a degree of formal assessment. But this sits comfortably alongside the involvement of the all-important consumer, whose opinions now count for plenty in the search for winners.

> **The most significant development has been the welcome inclusion of more game foods on the nation's restaurant menus. This has necessitated a complete redefinition of what constitutes 'wild' in terms of the Challenge criteria.**

Arguably the most significant development has been the welcome inclusion of more game foods on the nation's restaurant menus. This has necessitated a complete redefinition of what constitutes 'wild' in terms of the Challenge criteria.

Ingredients that not so long ago were perceived as 'wild foods', including possum, tahr, boar, hare and pheasant, are now reasonably commonplace so that participating chefs have to work much harder at coming up with something unusual. In the current Challenge context 'wild' can still mean something non-farmed but it can also mean an unconventional cooking method, an unusual presentation, an unexpected combination of ingredients and even a mix of all of the above!

The clever people at Monteith's realized early on that, aside from the difficulties facing the chefs, it would take something quite special to coax diners to try the often obscurely named

Challenge dishes and the accompanying beers. Monteith's could see that making the experience fun for diners would go a long way towards solving this problem. And so it was decided to award significant marks for service delivery and the clear demonstration of an understanding of the Challenge, along with a preparedness to go to the necessary lengths to get diners to participate. Dressing up the restaurant and having staff wear appropriately wild clothing became commonplace. For example, in the very early days of the Challenge, an Auckland chef and restaurant owner, also a keen tramper and hunter, turned part of his restaurant into a rainforest — even garnishing his dishes with .22-calibre bullets. Needless to say, the Occupational Safety and Health people were not too impressed, but it was great publicity for the Challenge. Then there was the high-class restaurant in a suburb of Christchurch where white tablecloths and a highly formal approach were the norm. One particular year they used a duck whistle rather than the traditional bell to let the waiters know that meals were ready.

> **Over the years, the true success of the Challenge has been the willingness of the Kiwi dining public to put aside their preconceptions.**

Stuffed animals, greenery, camouflage netting, staff dressed in possum fur, peacock feathers and bushmen's singlets, bird calls, and insects for garnishes — you name it — one way or another they've all been incorporated into the presentation of the Challenge menus.

Possibly the most extensive publicity for any one Challenge entrant was not even generated by the organizers. It came for the Hamilton Museum entry the year it served horse. Reports of the meal turned up in news bulletins in Eastern Europe, the United States, Australia, Fiji and Germany, as well as throughout New Zealand.

However, it hasn't all been plain sailing. Auckland, home to more restaurants and cafés than any other New Zealand city, has always been the most difficult market to enthuse. Unlike other more southern cities, Auckland has a less well-defined winter season and as such no real off-peak season when custom is hard to encourage. In addition, there is always so much else going on in Auckland that there are many more calls on a restaurant's resources. And perhaps the sheer amount of human resource it takes to participate in the Challenge is sometimes just too daunting for busy Auckland venues.

There was also a period when things got a little out of hand and the creativity shown by participants with both ingredient combinations and the names of their dishes trended towards the truly weird. As a result, we had to remind our entrants that this was a legitimate cooking competition and not a restaurant version of *Fear Factor*!

Over the years, the true success of the Challenge has been the willingness of the Kiwi dining public to put aside their preconceptions. They enter into the spirit of the Challenge by eschewing the ubiquitous chicken, beef and pork in favour of something significantly wilder and therefore challenging. Of course, the risk has always been that you may be served with a dish that takes you right out your culinary comfort zone.

But that willingness to walk the boundaries of the dining experience has been the essence of the surprise, the fun and, ultimately, the success of the Challenge.

The opportunity to participate in the annual Challenge, now called the Monteith's Beer and Wild Food Challenge in acknowledgement of the important part beer plays in the process, is coveted by many of the country's best restaurants, some of which have been involved since its earliest days.

So is there any real challenge in the Challenge any more? Without a doubt! The skill of beer and food matching is a culinary art that has been around for centuries and deserves much more attention than it has had until now. More than anything else, the Monteith's Beer and Wild Food Challenge encourages this development while giving the New Zealand diner something truly different to savour.

Now you, the competent Kiwi cook taking your lead from the recipes in this book, have the opportunity to test your own ability at matching beer and food. When you hit upon a successful match, it can be a wonderful experience. Most importantly, the excitement it will introduce into your kitchen will forever make you think differently about your approach to creating interesting food.

It will, dare I say it, give you a much greater understanding of the skills honed to such sharpness by those who for the last 15 wonderful years have courageously taken on the Monteith's Beer and Wild Food Challenge.

Monteith's Brewing Company

A heritage best remembered

In the mid- to late 1800s 'new' New Zealanders were busy taming the land. It was hard work; long hours of back-breaking toil felling and clearing, growing what they could to furnish the meal table, and in some areas extracting for profit any riches they could, mostly gold and coal.

MR. STEWART MONTEITH.

The West Coast of the South Island proved fertile ground not just for farmers, miners and loggers, but for grocers and blacksmiths as well. In addition to their labour they shared a common need: beer. Beer to slake the thirst, to distract them from the constant grind and, most importantly, to provide a reason to come together to share stories, memories and dreams.

And there were plenty of brewers and publicans willing to fill the need, especially on the West Coast. In 1886, for instance, a count revealed over a hundred pubs in Hokitika, with 87 on the main street alone, and three breweries. Greymouth had one brewery and 56 pubs and there were even three pubs in Blackball.

One of those brewers was Stewart Monteith. He had moved up from Otago and settled in Reefton, where he took over the reins of the Phoenix Brewery in 1868.

Monteith had something of a chequered past. In Otago he was hauled before the courts after complaints he'd been running an illegal brewing operation. He was convicted and fined £3. Monteith declared he was unable to pay and so spent six weeks in the slammer.

The heady days of beer and the West Coast were not to last. Changing fortunes in the goldfields and coal mines had led to a decline in the population. Throughout the country, the temperance movement was making a lot of noise, and in 1917 the government introduced six o'clock closing for pubs, with a total ban on liquor sales on Sundays. Just for the duration of the war, you understand … And then in 1919 a referendum to ban the sale and consumption of alcohol altogether was narrowly defeated, with 49.7 per cent of voters actually thinking prohibition would be a good idea. Luckily, 50.3 per cent of the voters — level-headed and clear-thinking people all — prevailed.

Still, the writing was on the wall. By 1927 there were a mere 16 pubs in Hokitika and just 21 in Greymouth. Five of the surviving breweries on the Coast got together and formed the Westland Brewing Co., led by Phoenix head William Patrick Monteith, son of Stewart. The other breweries were Klappe and Kortegast Brewery, Mandl's Brewery and Davies Bros. (Crown) Brewery in Hokitika, and Pearn's Brewery of Kumara.

The head office was built on a new site in Greymouth, where Monteith's is still brewed today, but the lack of a decent source

> **In addition to their labour they shared a common need: beer. Beer to slake the thirst, to distract them from the constant grind and, most importantly, to provide a reason to come together to share stories, memories and dreams.**

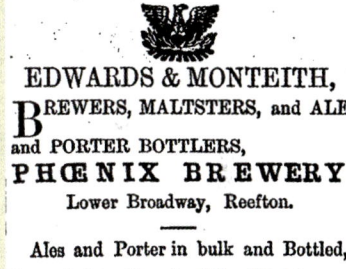

ABOVE An advertisement from the *Inangahua Times*, 16 October 1882. *Monteith's Archive.*

OPPOSITE Stewart Monteith took over the Phoenix Brewery in Reefton in 1878. *Monteith's Archive.*

NEXT PAGE J. Mandl and Co. Brewery, Hokitika, c.1890. *Barry Thompson Collection, Alexander Turnbull Library.*

of well water made brewing on-site impractical at that stage.

But, as they say on the Coast, there are no such things as problems, just new situations. So until that situation was rectified, the beers were brewed at their original breweries and trucked through to Greymouth in wooden hogsheads, each holding 54 gallons or nearly 250 litres.

In 1947, the New Zealand Government decreed that the price of a 10 oz glass of beer should rise by a penny. The beer-lovers in Greymouth decided it wouldn't and refused to enter any bar that put the price up. The strike lasted for several months and had two interesting outcomes: the birth of the workingmen's club on the West Coast (at first sly-grogging dens but later legitimized) and the phasing out of 10 oz glasses in pubs.

> **In 1947, the New Zealand Government decreed that the price of a 10 oz glass of beer should rise by a penny. The beer-lovers in Greymouth decided it wouldn't and refused to enter any bar that put the price up.**

Gradually over the years new facilities were added to Greymouth, meaning brewing could start there, and several of the older turn-of-the-century breweries were closed down. Beer was then trucked in the other direction, still in wooden hogsheads up until the early 1960s when aluminium kegs, known in the trade as 'alumus' were introduced.

For the drivers, rolling the kegs off the trucks could be a tricky business, with a keg likely to split open if it rolled too fast and hit something. To get around this they carried an old sugar bag filled with used cork bungs to provide cushioning. The old bag was known as a 'mother-in-law' for reasons that have long been forgotten.

In 1959 there was a major change in brewing methods, from 'naturally conditioned beer', where some fermentation continues in the bottle to give it that fizz, and some sediment, to 'chilled carbonated beer' where the fizz is added and the sediment left out altogether. New chilling and refrigeration was installed at Greymouth and the brewing process improved at Hokitika, while brewing was discontinued at Reefton.

The foundations of the Phoenix Brewery in Reefton can still be found, however, near the stables at Reefton Racecourse. And, if you look carefully, you might be able to find some of the descendants of the hops they used growing wild nearby.

In the 1960s the Westland Breweries family welcomed two new arrivals: Morley's Brewery in Westport and Harley's Brewery

MR. W. P. MONTEITH.

ABOVE In 1927 four of the surviving breweries on the Coast got together and formed the Westland Brewing Co., led by Phoenix head William Patrick Monteith. *Monteith's Archive.*

OPPOSITE The Denniston Hotel, 1945. *John Pascoe Collection, Alexander Turnbull Library.*

in Nelson. Well, not exactly new — both could trace their beginnings back to the mid-1880s as well. There was now even more history in every drop of Westland beer.

Change was in the air, again. In 1967 the temporary wartime measure of six o'clock closing was repealed and replaced with a more sensible ten o'clock curfew. And around the same time Dominion Breweries, one of the country's Big Two, decided to look around for a presence on the West Coast. Negotiations started and in 1969 the takeover took place with the DB logo over the door of the Westland Brewing Co.

Westland Brewery still produced its own beers, though, with Westbrew Golden Lager, Tira Pale Ale, Westland Extra Stout, Morley's Special Stout and Monteith's Pale Ale among the favourites.

As the 1990s approached, beer consumption in New Zealand began to fall, although the number of small craft breweries started to grow. The staff of Westland Brewery began discussing the need for a new approach so that their quality beers could be enjoyed by a wider range of discerning beer drinkers.

> **Words like passion and loyalty and commitment flew hither and yon, and the advantages of having a signature brewery became very apparent. Monteith's was back, almost like a phoenix from the ashes.**

History showed that Monteith's was the core of what had been Westland Breweries. So back they went to 1927 and resurrected the earlier name of Monteith's Brewing Company. They also brought back the family of beers representing the history of the breweries on the West Coast, to give New Zealand beer-lovers a clear picture of what the beers produced by the Greymouth brewery represented. And to give just as clear a beer, 1995 saw the bottling operation fitted with a sterile filter line so bottles could be filled without pasteurizing.

The new millennium started with a bit of a hiccup, as DB's head office sought to rationalize core business and announced the imminent closure of its Greymouth operations. To say there was an outcry would be putting it mildly. Coasters were up in arms — something they had a history of doing; remember the 1947 beer strike — at the prospect of their brewery, their beer and their contribution to New Zealand's history disappearing.

Words like passion and loyalty and commitment flew hither and yon, and the advantages of having a signature brewery became very apparent. Monteith's was back, almost

OPPOSITE At the Greymouth brewery wooden hogsheads were used up until the 1960s. *Monteith's Archive.*

NEXT PAGE Greymouth. *Monteith's Archive.*

like a phoenix from the ashes. Today, this heritage of brewing continues in Greymouth with small batches — as small as 70 hectolitres a brew, around 3000 six-packs — fermented in gyles, which are traditional open-topped vessels. Nothing gets between the brewers and the beer.

The ability to craft smaller batches gives Monteith's an edge. Along with the stable of regulars like Pilsner, Black, Golden and Original, there are regular seasonal brews like Summer Ale and Winter Ale. Beer-lovers look forward to the change of season to see what surprises might be in store.

There was also one very special batch brewed for an American couple. They'd got engaged in New Zealand, toasting each other with a glass of Monteith's, and couldn't fathom their wedding in Minnesota without a generous supply of fine Monteith's beer.

In one and a half centuries the Monteith's family of naturally brewed beers has received numerous awards. While they call themselves 'Proud Brewer to the West Coast', success has been international. In 1996 Monteith's beers emerged from the Australian International Brewing Awards with a gold medal, later to be chosen as Top Ale and then triumphing as the Best Beer overall (open section champion). In 1999 Monteith's was chosen as Champion Brewery for the highest aggregate score across all of its beers.

Today, Monteith's operates as a distinct company, while taking advantage of the vast resources of the larger DB Breweries.

Brewers to the Coast, and to the rest of the world, Monteith's unpasteurized, quality crafted beers offer taste beyond the ordinary. That's because there's history in the making.

Timeline of Monteith's

Monteith's has been crafting its family of fine beers for nigh on 150 years. In fact, the history of Monteith's and the history of the West Coast go pretty much hand in hand.

1860s

Proper beer, made from hops and malt, proves far more successful. Prospectors flock to the West Coast, followed closely by grocers, blacksmiths and brewers.

1889

Beer is big business. There are 105 hotels in Hokitika (87 on one street) and three breweries. Greymouth has 56 hotels and one brewery.

1773

Captain James Cook brews New Zealand's first beer from molasses, rimu and manuka. The beer cures scurvy but fails to ignite interest in pub franchise.

1868

When it all started. Stewart Monteith buys into the Phoenix Brewery in Reefton.

1917

Six o'clock closing for pubs is introduced as a 'temporary measure'. Temporary in this case means 50 years as the law isn't repealed until 1967.

LEFT TO RIGHT Criterion Hotel, Greymouth, c.1900. *Alexander Turnbull Library.*

Joseph Mandl, c.1890. *W.F. Heinz Collection, Alexander Turnbull Library.*

Revington's Hotel, Greymouth, c.1890. *Alexander Turnbull Library.*

Greymouth, 1951. *Whites Aviation Collection, Alexander Turnbull Library.*

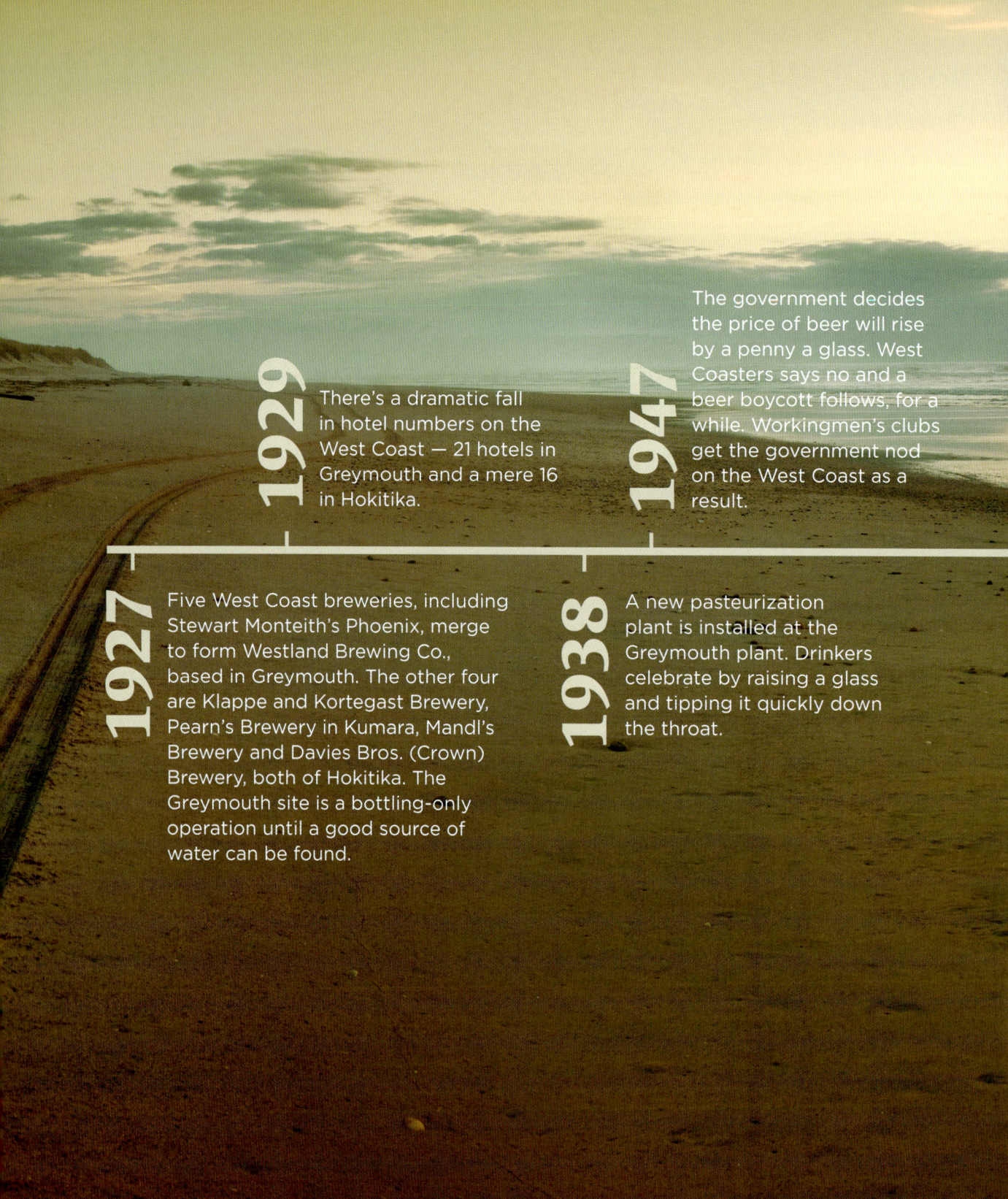

1929
There's a dramatic fall in hotel numbers on the West Coast — 21 hotels in Greymouth and a mere 16 in Hokitika.

1947
The government decides the price of beer will rise by a penny a glass. West Coasters says no and a beer boycott follows, for a while. Workingmen's clubs get the government nod on the West Coast as a result.

1927
Five West Coast breweries, including Stewart Monteith's Phoenix, merge to form Westland Brewing Co., based in Greymouth. The other four are Klappe and Kortegast Brewery, Pearn's Brewery in Kumara, Mandl's Brewery and Davies Bros. (Crown) Brewery, both of Hokitika. The Greymouth site is a bottling-only operation until a good source of water can be found.

1938
A new pasteurization plant is installed at the Greymouth plant. Drinkers celebrate by raising a glass and tipping it quickly down the throat.

1959 New chilling and refrigeration is installed at Greymouth. Brewing is discontinued in Reefton but carries on, with improved systems, at Hokitika. Fermented beer is transported to the Greymouth plant, where new glass lines and tanks have also been installed.

1967 A Steinecker Hydro Brewhouse plant arrives in Greymouth and the brewhouse at Hokitika is closed.

1955 Uranium is discovered on the West Coast. Hopes of a new atom bomb industry to revitalize the region fade after scientists find there's only enough for one luminous watch.

1960 Aluminium kegs are introduced to replace wooden barrels.

1969 On 1 April Westland Breweries Ltd buys Morley's Brewery in Westport and Harley's in Nelson. Dominion Breweries Ltd successfully negotiates a takeover of Westland Breweries Ltd.

1987

Upgrading of the Monteith's site begins, and lasts for three years.

1995

A new bottling line with a sterile filter system is installed, which means there's now no need for pasteurization — just clean clear beer in every bottle. Or keg. Or glass . . .

1990

A change of brewery name for the new decade — Westland becomes Monteith's, and traditional brews are reintroduced to reflect the historic origins of the brewery.

1999

Worldwide success! Monteith's receives the Grande Gold award at the prestigious Monde Brewing Awards in Brussels, and is voted Champion Brewery in Australasia at the Australian International Brewing Awards the very same year.

MONTEITH'S
BREWING CO

2001

On 22 March DB reviews its brewing operations and decides to close Monteith's Brewery.

2011

Work begins on refreshing Monteith's Brewery in Greymouth. A whole new look is in the offing, with much better facilities — including a café and tasting room — for the tens of thousands of visitors each year.

2001

On 26 March DB announces that the Monteith's brand is too important to the Coast, and the country, to lose. Over 130 years of history and strong support from the community win the day and the Monteith's West Coast brewery reopens.

2012

The new improved Monteith's Brewery opens, with brand-new equipment that makes the brewery one of the most modern in the world. The beer, though, will remain the same — staying true to the authentic process and recipes of the classic beer varieties. But that's probably something you'll need to check out for yourself.

Beer and food

Beer remains a key element in much of our conviviality and our entertainment; it is almost always present at social gatherings involving celebration and commemoration. The bigger breweries, as well as touting their products, have continued to support community activities, sponsoring sport and cultural endeavours, and have been both courted and criticized for their efforts.

Craft brews are increasingly visible and the range of products continues to grow. Among the beers available in New Zealand are brands that will last only until someone tastes them, and we have beers that have repeatedly won the highest international accolades. We have quaffers, we have speciality beers, we have high-strength and low-strength, hand-made and mass-produced. The journey through the world should take in beers from the entire spectrum, but there is no doubt that a great place to begin is with the beers that have largely been responsible for bringing to our attention the natural link between food and beer — Monteith's.

The concept is simple: if you choose the right beer to accompany the right food, your enjoyment of both will be enhanced.

The serving of beer with food is neither new nor peculiar. Brewhouses, cafés and wayside inns have been around for centuries and they have always, always involved food. Wherever beer is served in Europe you see counter lunches, pies, ploughman's lunches, biersticks, beer batter, beer bread, pizza and so on. You only have to look at the art of Bruegel and other European masters to see how often the tankard of ale was set down beside the

> "
> **Good food and good beer form, in every sense of the word, a perfect marriage.**
> — PETER LA FRANCE, *COOKING AND EATING WITH BEER*
> "

roast game or the platter of bread and cheese. Basic, hearty fare was the order of the day, and while today the food options are much broader, the exploration of combinations remains valid. Recognition of this comes in the ever-expanding library of books on beer and food from authors all around the world.

Beer drinkers' palates are changing and developing, becoming more sensitive as tasters become more knowledgeable. In general, we are taking more time to sample and savour different brands, to appreciate the style and aroma, to distinguish between flavours and to appreciate the craftsmanship that provides strong, individual characteristics in each beer. A logical step in this process is making beer a valid option when looking for a beverage to accompany and enhance meals.

Get to know something about beer. Learn to distinguish a lager from a Pilsner, a Guinness from a stout. Find out more about brewing and the processes that contribute to the taste profiles. Build up a vocabulary of appropriate terms so that, when discussing beer, you are able to share your thoughts about the flavours you pick up.

When matching beer with food there are some important things to keep in mind. It can be as complex, as tantalizing, varied and exciting as matching wine and food. As with wine matching, no one beer will combine with all food in a way that satisfies everyone's palate. Most beers go with most food, but finding a superb beer and food match is more of a challenge. The quest is for synergy; neither the beer nor the food should overwhelm the other. They should be better in combination than they are apart. Pairing beer and food is subjective, but there are some clear rules that will assist those thinking of giving it a go.

It is likely that beer styles from certain regions will combine best with the cuisine styles of the same region. There is good reason for this. Craft brewers have been the rule, not the exception, around the world, so beer — until the advent of modern transportation — has always had a strong regional connection. Beer was made in small batches by home and village brewers, and these craftsmen used local ingredients and were subject to local brewing conditions. Consequently the flavour of these beers reflected the local environment or *terroir*, to borrow a hip winemaking term.

In this way the development of beer has mirrored that of cuisine. But while there has been an enormous increase in the acceptance of international brands, many beers still have their greatest support close to home. It is logical therefore to look first at local cuisine to find what scope there is for finding that ideal combination.

Now, as with wine, there is a huge element of personal preference in all this. There are no right or wrong answers. However, to get the best out of the experience it is worth taking time to consider what makes a better-than-average combination.

The tasting

All styles of beer have completely individual textures, aromas and flavours. They all affect the palate differently and our senses react to each of them differently. Every beer is made using a unique recipe and between them they cover every element and facet of the flavour spectrum.

So get to know something about beer. Learn to distinguish a lager from a Pilsner (also known as Pilsener or Pils), a Guinness from a stout. Find out more about brewing and the processes that contribute to the taste profiles. Build up a vocabulary of appropriate terms so that, when discussing beer, you are able to share your thoughts about the flavours you pick up.

Get in the habit of presenting a beer at its best. The temperature generally should be 6–8°C, although typically in New Zealand beer is drunk at around 3–4°C. Serve a good-quality beer in a good-quality glass. While appearance is not strictly important when matching a beer with food, it is part of the enjoyment to see the appropriate colour, clarity and head for the beer style. The glass should be clear and cleaned of any soap residue.

Aroma is very important because our sense of smell is so closely tied into our sense of taste. Take time to lift the glass to your nose and form an opinion as to what fragrances you can identify. Common characteristics are the flowery and herbal nose of a well-brewed lager and the maltiness of a Bavarian-style beer. Often ales leave an impression of fruitiness.

Flavour, naturally, is the most important characteristic. Taking into account the influence of each ingredient and the particular beer style on the final product will definitely aid in the food-matching process. Begin with a generous mouthful and swirl it around so that it covers all the palate before swallowing.

The 'body' of a beer, as with wine, ranges from thin to full with the same general matching principles. The perceived thickness of a beer comes from its grain to water ratio. Carbonation should also be considered because an overly effervescent beer hampers the ability of the palate to taste. Look for a smooth, elegant, complex finish and note whether it quickly disappears or lingers a little.

The matching

When pairing beer and food the choices are as complex as you want them to be, but the end result can be simply wonderful. Many beers make excellent aperitifs, as the bitterness produced by the hops stimulates the appetite by increasing the production of gastric juices. The chemistry of the mouth is changed a great deal by food and one's appreciation of the beer changes accordingly. The main thing is to keep it simple — match like with like.

When considering a menu for your guests, think about dishes that emphasize wholesome, natural ingredients in keeping with the entirely natural ingredients and processing involved in the making of beer. Try to achieve a high degree of compatibility between the beer and the menu in terms of texture, flavour and balance.

The less sweet the food, the drier the beer should be. Pair a delicate shellfish dish with a pale ale or mild lager, which are made using light and subtle ingredients. If you increase the seasoning or choose more strongly flavoured ingredients, the beer should also be more intense, perhaps an amber ale or dark lager. Darker beers — porters and stouts — all beautifully balance red meats in rich sauces and gravies. They also go well with savoury spiced meats like corned beef or the traditional roast.

Beer is a perfect foil for ethnic, especially spicy, cuisine. Water only spreads the chilli around, but it is tremendously refreshing to wash down hot food with a Pilsner, a light amber or mild wheat beer. The higher the alcohol content, the more soothing the beer will be.

OPPOSITE Tony Mercer, Monteith's head brewer, has been in the brewing business for 30 years.

Cooking with beer

The French and the Belgians are credited with developing the cooking style that uses beer as a key ingredient. This is hardly surprising given the close proximity between a nation of passionate foodies and a nation of equally fanatical beer-lovers.

According to drinks writer Michael Jackson in his *Beer Companion* (Running Press, 1994), 'Bellot was holding monthly banquets featuring dishes made from beer as early as the 1870s.' Since those very early days, Belgian and French chefs, including some very illustrious names, have taken the art form to extraordinary heights.

But neither nationality can claim to be the only promoters of cuisine *à la bière*. Cooks in the United States are creating wonderful recipes using beer, as are chefs in other European countries. In Australia and New Zealand, too, there are groups of chefs who delight in experimenting with adding beer to their favourite dishes. In fact, the addition of beer into cooking is happening throughout the foodie world, not as a replacement for wine but as an alternative expression of what it is possible for beverages to contribute.

A quick check on the web reveals that many books on the subject of cooking with beer have already been published and that each year the list grows with new and established authors contributing their favourite recipes and ideas.

The wonderful thing about using beer in cooking is that you can produce meals that are highly complex and sophisticated or you can serve up something simple but equally delicious. And, provided you follow a few simple guidelines, beer can be used successfully in any course. It can be used as a marinade, in soups, casseroles and even desserts. It can also be used as a base or as a flavour supplement in breads, sauces and mustards. You can use it as your cooking medium, for example, to steam open shellfish, and you can use it to tenderize meat.

Beer has the added advantage of being less expensive than wine, but there is a cautionary note here: in the same way that cooking with undrinkable wine will spoil food, so will using poor quality beer produce less satisfactory results in your dishes. So choose prudently.

On a more positive note, serving either the same or a similar beer to the one you have used in your recipe works just as well as serving the same wine you cooked with.

Are there many advantages of beer over wine? In certain circumstances the answer is yes. Beer is much less acidic than the wine, vinegar or citrus juices you might use in your marinades, so it will tenderize meats more gently than some of the more traditional agents. If this is managed well it can lead to a better balance between ingredients and there is less chance that, say, herbs or sugars will be overwhelmed by any residual acidity. This makes beer, especially the darker maltier beers, an ideal choice for marinades or sauces for barbecued meats where you want that rich sweetish coat to contrast with the smokiness that comes from the fire.

> **The rules are fairly straightforward. Where you might use a white wine or an ingredient that adds acidity, use a lager or Pilsner. When you might add a red wine for texture and sweetness, then opt for a malty beer or porter.**

Beer contributes a number of flavour elements to cooking: the hoppy lagers and Pilsners will add bitterness and often a herbaceous character, although typically this is more subtle. Darker beers offer sweeter flavours from the malts, while yeasty beers contribute a bready character. Often a wheat beer with its citrus and clove characters can add a further interesting dimension to the sauce you add to barbecued shellfish or seafood. Beer can also add to the aroma of your dish.

But you still need to be careful in selecting the right beer for each dish. For example, as beer heats up and reduces, the sweetness intensifies and it can become syrupy. This may not be the effect you seek, so malty or dark beer may not be appropriate. Another example is the 'off' flavours that can derive from fruity beer when heated. These may work with stronger gamey meats but not with seafood. Highly hopped beers do nothing for dishes that require boiling or simmering for lengthy periods. They can become stale-tasting and result in a cooked cabbage stench in your kitchen.

The rules are fairly straightforward. Where you might use a white wine or an ingredient that adds acidity, use a lager or Pilsner. When you might add a red wine for texture and sweetness, then opt for a malty beer or porter. If it's the flavours of a sherry or port you want to create, then consider a stout or a fruity Lambic beer as a substitute.

Finally, think carefully about when you should add beer to your cooking to achieve optimum results. Like wine, beer changes when heated and evaporation in a dish can lead to an intensification of flavour. If it's subtlety you are after then you can add it later, but if you want the full force of the beer's contribution to permeate your food then earlier is better.

The number and variety of Monteith's beers available from your supermarket means there is ample opportunity to experiment. Be prepared to substitute beer for another ingredient in your favourite dishes and then move on to develop new and exciting flavour combinations using beer as a core ingredient. It can be tremendous fun and makes for great conversation at the dinner table.

MAINS

BOAR BURGER

2 large white onions
1 kg boar mince
1 kg lean beef mince
2 cups fine wholemeal
   breadcrumbs
¼ cup sweet soy sauce
   (a thick-consistency sauce
   is recommended)
¼ cup sweet chilli sauce
2 eggs
salt and pepper
fresh wholemeal burger buns
   (or use the brioche recipe on
   page 202)
mayonnaise
mustard pickle
lettuce
tomato
radish
Cheddar or blue vein cheese

A simple, succulent burger perfect for any day's lunch or Sunday dinner. These patties will freeze well or last in the fridge, covered, for 2–3 days. Use wild boar or good-quality pork mince. Beef mince is also used, as boar mince is too lean to bind well on its own.

ACCOMPANIED WITH MONTEITH'S PILSNER

Dice the onions very finely and combine with the boar mince, beef mince, breadcrumbs, soy sauce, sweet chilli sauce, eggs and seasoning in a large bowl. Mix well. Press the mixture tightly into a 10 cm steel ring mould. When it is full, gently release the mould. Repeat the process until all the mixture is used. Heat the oven to 170°C. Bake the patties on an oven tray lined with baking paper for approximately 45 minutes or until just cooked through. Allow to cool on a baking rack to help set the patties.

ASSEMBLY

Reheat the patties under the grill or over a medium heat on your barbecue, making sure the patties are turned often to prevent burning. Allow just long enough for the centre of the patties to become hot. Place a patty in a wholemeal burger bun with mayonnaise, mustard pickle, lettuce, tomato, radish and aged Cheddar or blue vein cheese.

ARANCINI À LA MER

2 tbsp canola oil

1 medium brown onion, finely
chopped

2 cloves garlic, thinly sliced

10 g red chilli, chopped

1 cup Arborio rice

1 litre lemon-infused vegetable
stock (see page 221)

1 cup raw prawn meat,
chopped

10 g butter

10 g coriander, chopped

20 g Parmesan, grated

salt and pepper

1 cup flour

2 eggs

1 cup milk

2 cups breadcrumbs

PESTO

1 bunch spinach

1 bunch coriander

salt and pepper

40 ml white wine vinegar
(or lemon juice)

80 g peanuts, toasted

20 ml sesame oil

60 ml canola oil

breadcrumbs

Prawn and chilli rice balls with coriander and spinach pesto.

ACCOMPANIED WITH MONTEITH'S GOLDEN LAGER

Heat half the canola oil and sauté the onion over a medium heat until it starts to turn transparent. Add the garlic and chilli and cook for a further 3 minutes over a low heat. Add the remaining oil, add the rice and warm through, coating the rice in the hot onion and garlic oil, for another 2–3 minutes, stirring so as not to burn the rice. Start adding the stock slowly, a ladleful at a time, continuously stirring the rice as it will boil straight away. Continue to add the stock until you have added 750 ml. If the rice is still too crunchy, a little more stock may be needed. Add the prawn meat and butter. It will take only a few seconds to cook. Take off the heat and spread onto a flat tray to cool.

Once the risotto is cooled, place it in a bowl with the chopped coriander, Parmesan and seasoning. Place the flour, eggs and milk beaten together, and the breadcrumbs in three separate bowls. Roll the risotto mix into small golf-ball-sized balls. Dip each one first in the flour, then the egg mixture and lastly the crumbs. Place on a baking tray and bake at 200°C for 15 minutes.

CORIANDER AND SPINACH PESTO

Wash the spinach well to remove any soil. De-stem the coriander and spinach and place in a bowl of cold water with salt and vinegar or lemon juice. Drain in a strainer, ensuring most of the liquid has gone.

Place all the ingredients except the breadcrumbs in a food processor. Blend well — this could take 3–5 minutes — into a thick, smooth paste. Use the breadcrumbs to get the pesto to the desired texture, adding them slowly and turning the blender on and off. Season the mixture as you go to get the taste you like.

ASSEMBLY

Serve the warm arancini with a bowl of coriander and spinach pesto on the side as a dipping sauce.

DUCK AMONGST THE FRUIT

canola oil

2 litres vegetable stock

500 g polenta

70 g Parmesan, grated

salt and pepper

2 cinnamon quills

2 star anise

100 g soft brown sugar

100 g salt

4 medium duck legs

2 oranges, sliced

1 kg duck fat

wilted spinach

orange coulis (see page 224)

raspberry vincotto (available
   from Mediterranean food
   stockists)

*Confit duck with polenta chips, spinach, orange coulis and raspberry
vincotto. Note that your polenta and duck will need to rest overnight
before serving.*

ACCOMPANIED WITH MONTEITH'S CELTIC RED

Grease a 30 cm square tray with canola oil and line with baking paper. Bring the vegetable stock to the boil. Once boiled, add the polenta slowly, stirring at the same time so as not to let it catch on the bottom of the pot. Once all the polenta is in, add the Parmesan (the mixture should be quite firm). Season to taste. Place on the lined tray and smooth out with the back of a wooden spoon. Leave overnight to set. Once set, turn onto a chopping board and cut into chips. Refrigerate until needed.

In a mortar and pestle (or a food processor) take one cinnamon quill and one star anise and grind down. Add the sugar and salt and grind down more. Take the duck legs and cut an inch below the knuckle down to the bone of each leg, going right around the leg bone, making sure you cut the tendon. (This will make the skin pull back to the thigh during cooking and you will be able to remove the knuckle for presentation.) Coat the legs generously in the spiced sugar and salt rub. Arrange most of the orange slices on a plate and sit the duck on top, and place the remaining slices of orange on top of the legs. Cover and refrigerate overnight for at least 12 hours.

Preheat the oven to 180°C. Warm the duck fat to room temperature. Remove the orange slices and wash the legs in cold water; pat the duck dry with a paper towel. Place the duck legs in a shallow braising tray, and add the duck fat, extra cinnamon quill and star anise. Cover with baking paper and tinfoil. Cook for 10 minutes, then turn the oven down to 160°C for a further 45 minutes or until tender. Cool and leave in the fat until needed. This will preserve the legs for a week as long as no meat or bone is exposed to the open air.

Continued . . .

When ready to serve, preheat the oven to 200°C. Line an oven tray with baking paper and place the duck legs on the tray with the polenta chips. Cook for 8 minutes or until golden brown.

ASSEMBLY

Arrange the polenta chips on a heated plate and top with wilted spinach and the duck. Drizzle with orange coulis and raspberry vincotto.

RAUKUMARA RED

salt

4 venison shanks

1 tbsp allspice

1 tbsp juniper berries

8 cloves

1 cinnamon quill

1 dried hot chilli

2 bay leaves

1 tbsp black peppercorns

1 bottle red wine

2 tbsp molasses

1 tbsp olive oil

4 rashers bacon

2 onions, chopped

2 cloves garlic, chopped

2 cups venison stock (or beef stock)

kumara and parsnip mash, to serve

watercress or green beans

Venison shanks in red wine on sweet potato mash. Ask your butcher for front shanks. We use venison from the Raukumara Range, East Coast.

ACCOMPANIED WITH MONTEITH'S BLACK OR SINGLE SOURCE LAGER

Salt the shanks and set aside. Combine the spices and herbs with the wine and molasses in a shallow ovenproof dish or Dutch oven. Cover and cook on a low to medium heat. Do not allow the wine to go past a gentle simmer.

Preheat the oven to 160°C. In a frying pan, heat the olive oil on a medium setting. Fry the bacon slowly until crispy, turning often. As each rasher turns crispy, put it in the pot with the wine. Next, brown each surface of the shanks then place them in the pot — bones up — with the spices and wine (saving ½ cup). Using the same frying pan, caramelize the onions and garlic over a high heat. Deglaze the pan with the remaining wine, making sure to scrape everything off the bottom of the pan. Bring to a vigorous boil. Add this reduction to the wine pot, mixing with the stock. Be sure the shanks are still bone up. Cover and cook in the oven for 3–4½ hours depending on the shank size.

When the meat is nearly falling off the bone, gently remove and keep warm. Remove the bay leaves, cinnamon quill, chilli and as many cloves, peppercorns and juniper berries as you reasonably can.

ASSEMBLY

Serve with kumara and parsnip mash with the reduction poured liberally over the shanks. Garnish with fresh watercress or serve with steamed green beans.

STEWED ON CIDER

4 rabbit legs
2 cloves garlic, chopped
2 tbsp olive oil
1 sprig rosemary leaves,
  chopped
1 onion, diced
½ leek, sliced
2 fennel bulbs, sliced
1 stick celery, chopped
1 apple, peeled and diced
2 tbsp potato flour
  (or cornflour)
1 bottle Monteith's Crushed
  Apple Cider
200 ml chicken stock

CHESTNUT DUMPLINGS
100 g flour
1 tsp baking powder
50 g suet
75 g chestnuts, peeled
  and chopped
½ tsp salt
about 75 ml cold water

two bowl bread (see
  page 202)

Rabbit hotpot with cider and rosemary.

ACCOMPANIED WITH MONTEITH'S ORIGINAL

Remove the bones from the rabbit legs and cut the meat into small pieces. Combine the garlic, oil and rosemary. Rub the mixture over the meat, cover and refrigerate for 6–24 hours.

Preheat the oven to 160°C. In a frying pan sear the meat until coloured on each side. Put the meat in a pot with the onion, leek, fennel, celery and apple. Stir in the potato flour or cornflour. Add the cider and chicken stock, cover with a lid and bring to the boil.

To make the dumplings, mix the flour, baking powder, suet, chestnuts and salt together. Add enough water to bring the mix together to make
a dough. Form the dough into walnut-sized dumplings and place on top of the hotpot mix. Bake uncovered in the oven for 45 minutes.

ASSEMBLY

Serve in large preheated dinner bowls. This is delicious served with thick slices of homemade bread.

TAHR BABY

10 large prawns

350 g sweetbreads, washed and trimmed

4 egg whites

1 tbsp coriander, roughly chopped

chilli flakes, to taste

salt

freshly cracked black pepper

smoke mix (see page 212)

2 tahr racks

2 large kumara

2 cinnamon quills

2 sprigs thyme

2 cups white wine

butter

sweet chilli sauce, to taste

2 Shanghai cabbages, washed and trimmed

200 ml good-quality jus

Smoked tahr and sweetbread chorizo with Shanghai cabbage. Substitute goat, mutton or lamb for the tahr.

ACCOMPANIED WITH MONTEITH'S CELTIC RED

Shell and de-vein the prawns. Place half in a food processor with the sweetbreads and egg whites, and blend until a gooey paste forms. Roughly chop the remaining prawns (this adds texture) and, in a bowl, combine with the sweetbread mix. To this mixture add the coriander and chilli flakes, then season and mix well. Spoon the mixture onto plastic wrap that has been layered three times and roll into a sausage shape. Hold the shape using string or small rubber bands. Blanch in boiling salted water for around 5 minutes or until cooked.

Place the smoke mix on one side of a large sheet of tinfoil. Fold the foil to make a pouch and prick with something sharp to create holes on one side for the smoke to escape. Place in a heavy-bottomed pan over a high heat. Place the tahr on a rack over the foil package. When smoke appears, cover the pan with tinfoil and leave on the heat for 5 minutes. Then remove from the heat and put aside to rest.

While the tahr is smoking, peel and cut each of the kumara into large cubes. Place in a saucepan with the cinnamon and half the thyme and cover with wine. Cook over a moderate heat until tender. Check often and once cooked set aside.

Seal the rested tahr in a hot ovenproof pan and place the remaining thyme on top. Roast in a 180°C oven for 5–8 minutes or until the juices run clear. Rest for 5 minutes. While the tahr is cooking, sauté the kumara in butter until golden round the edges. In a separate pan, sauté the sweetbread chorizo, adding a little sweet chilli sauce near the end. Blanch the Shanghai cabbage and heat the jus.

ASSEMBLY

Cut the racks of tahr into eight pieces and place one or two on each plate. Arrange the kumara, Shanghai cabbage and chorizo as desired. Spoon over the warmed jus and serve.

NEK MINUTE VENISON

½ cup balsamic vinegar

½ cup red wine

2 tbsp sugar

1 large potato, thinly sliced
  into rounds

50 g butter, melted

salt and pepper

2 medium apples

100 ml Monteith's Crushed
  Pear Cider

8 venison medallions

olive oil

rocket leaves

Venison medallions with roasted apple, potato galette and rocket salad, and a red wine and balsamic reduction.

ACCOMPANIED WITH MONTEITH'S ORIGINAL

Preheat the oven to 180°C. In a saucepan reduce the balsamic vinegar, red wine and sugar by half over a medium heat.

In a bowl toss together the potato slices, butter and seasoning. In four separate portions, arrange the potatoes overlapping each other in a circular fashion on a lined baking tray. Place in the oven for 15–20 minutes, then flip and cook for a further 5–10 minutes until golden and crispy.

While the potatoes are cooking, peel and core the apples and cut into 1 cm cubes. Place the apples and cider into an oven dish. Place in the oven for 10 minutes until the apples are soft. Ensure the apple cubes keep their shape.

Season the venison. Heat a pan and add a dash of olive oil. When the pan is hot, sear each side of the venison for 2–3 minutes. Remove from the heat and cover. Allow to rest for 2–3 minutes.

ASSEMBLY

Preheat four dinner plates. Divide the apple cubes into four servings and place a portion in the centre of each plate. Place two medallions on top of the apple. Serve with potato galette and garnish with a rocket salad. Drizzle with the red wine and balsamic reduction.

CAPTAIN COOKER

½ brown onion, finely diced
800 g wild boar mince
1 tsp ground horopito
2 eggs
2 tsp salt
1 tsp cracked pepper
½ cup white breadcrumbs
3 large red kumara
canola oil, for frying
4 brioche buns (see page 202)
butter
cider-braised onions (see
  page 207)
200 g Gruyère cheese
1 large head cos lettuce
4 large vine tomatoes
roasted beetroot (see
  page 207)
aioli (see page 214)

Gourmet boar burger with cider-braised onions and aioli, served with kumara chips.

ACCOMPANIED WITH MONTEITH'S CRUSHED APPLE CIDER

Cook the onion on a medium heat until soft. Allow to cool and then combine with the mince, horopito, eggs, seasonings and breadcrumbs in a bowl. Mix well and divide into four even portions. Roll into balls and flatten to form patties. Cover and refrigerate.

Peel the kumara and cut into batons about 3 cm wide. Place in a large pot with cold water and bring to the boil. Cook just until the kumara starts to soften, then drain and dry with paper towels.

Heat a large pan and fry the patties in a little oil for 30 seconds on each side, then place in a 175°C oven for 6–8 minutes. Cook the kumara chips by either oven-baking or shallow-frying until golden.

ASSEMBLY
Cut the brioche buns in half and butter both sides. On the top half add the braised onions and a slice of cheese, then put under the grill to melt the cheese. At the same time put the bottom half under the grill and lightly toast.

Build the burger from the bottom up, adding cos lettuce, sliced tomato seasoned with salt, beetroot slices and the patty. Place the top half of the bun with the braised onions and cheese on top of the stack. Serve with kumara chips seasoned with salt and pepper, and a large portion of aioli for dipping.

PORK FOR PRINCES

4 x 300 g free-range pork
cutlets
50 g harissa spice mix
salt
200 ml Monteith's Crushed
Apple Cider
200 ml beef stock
1 red apple
100 g baby leeks
kumara dauphinoise (see
page 211)
40 g honeycomb

Harissa-marinated free-range pork cutlet served on kumara dauphinoise, with poached apple, blanched baby leeks, honeycomb and cider jus. Harissa is a mix of spices originating in North Africa containing paprika, cumin, coriander and chilli pepper. Pre-mixed packets are available from most good supermarkets. The spiced pork cutlet is best prepared a day ahead to allow the flavours of the spices to infuse the meat.

ACCOMPANIED WITH MONTEITH'S PILSNER

Rub the pork cutlets with the harissa and set aside. Once the dauphinoise is ready to be plated, preheat the oven to 200°C. Pan-sear the pork cutlets on each side, season with salt, and put in the oven for 20–25 minutes or until the pork is cooked all the way through.

Place 100 ml of the cider in a saucepan and reduce by half. Add the beef stock and reduce again by half or until the stock has thickened and will stick nicely to the back of a spoon.

Peel and cut the apple into four, removing the core. Slice into strips and gently poach in the remainder of the cider until soft and almost transparent.

One minute before plating, blanch the baby leeks in seasoned water until soft and tender.

ASSEMBLY

Cut the dauphinoise into four even-sized pieces. Place one piece onto each plate and one pork cutlet on top of the dauphinoise. Add baby leeks and poached apple in a rustic style to the side of the pork, overlapping the dauphinoise, and drizzle with a hearty amount of cider jus. For the finishing touches add honeycomb and a sprig of herb to garnish.

FISHING FOR COMPLIMENTS

300 g scallops

1 small onion, diced

200 g white fish fillets (e.g. gurnard or blue cod)

1 small fennel bulb

150 g raw prawns

4 eggs

salt and pepper

100 ml whole cream

¼ cup chopped fresh herbs (e.g. coriander, parsley, basil)

zest of 1 lemon

500 ml whole milk

2 whole gurnard (average 600 g per fish), gutted and scaled

2 cups flour

3 oranges, zest and segments

500 g pre-prepared dukkah

olive oil

KIWIFRUIT SAUCE

5 gold kiwifruit

2 bottles Monteith's Golden Lager

3 tbsp manuka honey

rustic vegetables (see page 212)

watercress

Dukkah-and-citrus-crusted gurnard with scallop, prawn and fennel mousse served with chunky rustic vegetables, petite watercress salad and Monteith's Golden Lager and kiwifruit sauce.

ACCOMPANIED WITH MONTEITH'S GOLDEN LAGER

Place the scallops, onion, fish fillets, fennel bulb and prawns in a food processor and pulse four or five times. Add two eggs and seasoning. Add the cream and pulse to incorporate. Fold in the herbs and lemon zest.

To prepare the egg wash for the fish coating, whisk two eggs and the milk together. Fill the cavity of each gurnard with the prepared mousse. Secure the fish cavity with skewers, roll each fish in flour to coat, and then coat in the egg wash. Add the orange zest to the dukkah and coat the floured and egg-washed fish with the dukkah. Place the stuffed and crusted gurnard in the fridge for 30 minutes to firm up prior to cooking.

For the sauce, peel the kiwifruit, place in a saucepan with Monteith's Golden Lager and the honey and simmer to a slow boil. Purée and set aside.

Heat oil in a large frying pan, place the crusted gurnard in the pan and brown quickly on each side. Place in a 180°C oven and cook for approximately 25–35 minutes. The fish should be firm to the touch to ensure they are cooked through.

ASSEMBLY

Once the fish is cooked, remove from the oven and place on a large serving platter with lemon wedges. The rustic vegetables can be placed on individual plates along with the kiwifruit sauce. Add a nice bunch of watercress for a salad garnish, along with some orange segments, to each serving.

RAZORBACK CARNIVAL

PORK BELLY
1 carrot, chopped
1 onion, chopped
½ leek, sliced
2 sticks celery, sliced
1 bottle Monteith's Crushed
  Pear Cider
2 cinnamon quills
1 bunch thyme
3 tbsp salt
750 g free-range pork belly

FARCE
1 razorback boar rack (or pork
  rack)
25 g walnuts, crushed
1 egg
50 ml cream
50 g bacon
50 g pancetta, roughly
  chopped
½ tbsp thyme, chopped
½ tbsp sage, chopped
½ tsp ground cumin seeds
½ tsp ground coriander seeds
1 shallot, finely diced
25 g pistachios, chopped
¼ tsp white pepper
¾ tsp salt

TOFFEE PEAR
300 g sugar
red food colouring
1 pear
toothpicks

Roasted wild razorback boar with a pancetta and pistachio farce, cider-braised pork belly, and a toffee pear.

ACCOMPANIED WITH MONTEITH'S CELTIC RED OR CRUSHED PEAR CIDER

CIDER-BRAISED PORK BELLY
Place all the ingredients except the pork in a deep roasting tray. Poke some holes in the pork belly with a fork or a small knife. Place the pork in the tray and top up with water until covered. Cover with baking paper then tinfoil, and place into a 160°C oven. Cook for 4½ hours. Allow to cool slightly in the liquid and then remove and press between two trays in the fridge. Once chilled it can be trimmed and portioned ready for serving.

RAZORBACK BOAR AND PANCETTA FARCE
Trim all the fat and meat from the rack, leaving only the bones and main part of the loin. Cut the trimmed rack into cutlets and scrape the bones. Place the meat trim and fat in a food processor and blend until you have a paste.

Add the walnuts and egg and blend until well incorporated. Slowly add the cream and then the bacon and blend some more. Remove the mix from the food processor and add all the other ingredients. This is your farce.

Divide the farce evenly over the cutlets on one side and then wrap each tightly with plastic wrap, tying at each end. These need to be dropped into boiling water for 7–8 minutes then unwrapped and coloured in a hot pan. Then place them in a 200°C oven for about another 4 minutes. Rest for 5 minutes before serving.

TOFFEE PEAR
Place the sugar and enough water to moisten it in a saucepan and boil until light golden. Add a few drops of red food colouring. Dip the outside of the pot in cold water to stop it

Continued . . .

VEGETABLES
½ savoy cabbage, thinly
  shaved
butter
salt and pepper
12 baby carrots, peeled and
  cleaned around top

SAUCE
50 ml pear syrup
100 ml beef stock
50 g butter

spiced pear and ginger relish
  (see page 219)
parsnip purée (see page 208)

cooking further. Scoop pear flesh with a melon baller and dip in the caramel using a toothpick, holding until the caramel hardens.

VEGETABLES
Blanch the cabbage in hot salted water, then sauté it in a little butter and season with salt and black pepper. Cook the baby carrots in the same way but omit the black pepper.

SAUCE
Boil all ingredients together until they reach the desired consistency.

ASSEMBLY
Place a swipe of parsnip purée across the plate. Arrange the pork belly on top, lean the boar rack against the belly and place the vegetables around the meat. Garnish with the sauce, relish and the toffee pear.

COLOURS OF CENTRAL OTAGO

oil
4 duck breasts
300 ml manuka honey
250 ml milk
250 ml water
400 g lamb sweetbreads
160 g black quinoa
300 ml chicken stock
4 small orange carrots
4 small violet carrots
4 small yellow carrots
4 small violet beets
4 small yellow beets
4 pieces blood orange, flesh
  only

Pan-roasted duck breast and lamb sweetbreads with a warm salad of winter vegetables.

ACCOMPANIED WITH MONTEITH'S WINTER ALE

Sear all the surfaces of the duck in a hot pan with a little oil until golden. Paint the duck with the manuka honey and place in a 180°C oven. Cook until the juices run clear. In a saucepan, add the milk and water and simmer the sweetbreads for 15 minutes, taking care to keep a gentle simmer only. Rinse the quinoa and cook in the chicken stock until tender. To prepare the vegetables, peel and steam over water until al dente. Use a cloth to remove the skins.

ASSEMBLY

Divide the quinoa and vegetables between four heated dinner plates. Place a duck breast on each plate and garnish with the sweetbreads and any juices from the duck pan.

Beer and food matching

◄ **BOAR BURGER**
with
MONTEITH'S PILSNER

― ― ― ― ― ―

▶ **ARANCINI À LA MER**
with
MONTEITH'S GOLDEN LAGER

― ― ― ― ― ―

◄ **DUCK AMONGST THE FRUIT**
with
MONTEITH'S CELTIC RED

― ― ― ― ― ―

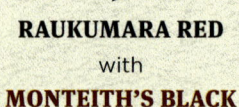

▶ **RAUKUMARA RED**
with
MONTEITH'S BLACK

― ― ― ― ― ―

◄ **STEWED ON CIDER**
with
MONTEITH'S ORIGINAL

― ― ― ― ― ―

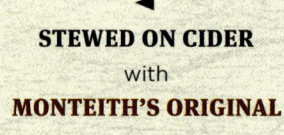

▶ **TAHR BABY**
with
MONTEITH'S CELTIC RED

― ― ― ― ― ―

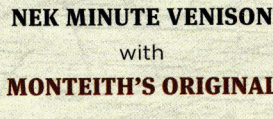

NEK MINUTE VENISON

with

MONTEITH'S ORIGINAL

▶

CAPTAIN COOKER

with

**MONTEITH'S CRUSHED
APPLE CIDER**

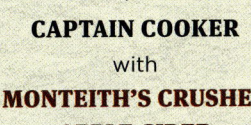

◀

PORK FOR PRINCES

with

MONTEITH'S PILSNER

▶

FISHING FOR COMPLIMENTS

with

MONTEITH'S GOLDEN LAGER

◀

RAZORBACK CARNIVAL

with

MONTEITH'S CELTIC RED

▶

COLOURS OF CENTRAL OTAGO

with

MONTEITH'S WINTER ALE

HONEY, THE DUCK'S SWEET ON THE SOW!

DUCK CONFIT

3 sprigs rosemary

3 sprigs thyme

1 head garlic, lightly crushed

5 tbsp flaky sea salt

½ tbsp black pepper

1 cinnamon quill

3 star anise

3 bay leaves

3 lime leaves

3 juniper berries

¼ cup sugar

4 duck legs

1 litre rendered duck fat

PORK BELLY

1 kg heritage breed saddleback
  (or best-quality) pork belly

olive oil

sea salt

black pepper

1 head garlic, skin on

1 bunch thyme

2½ cups white wine

250 g manuka honey

2 tbsp fresh ginger, grated

½ tbsp red chilli, finely
  chopped

½ cup onion, celery and carrot,
  roughly chopped

Honey-and-ginger-braised pork belly and confit duck leg, with caramelized orange, kumara fondant, chilli and lime syrup, and red onion and fennel salad. Note that the duck should marinate for 48 hours before cooking.

ACCOMPANIED WITH MONTEITH'S RADLER

DUCK CONFIT

In a tray large enough to hold the duck legs in a single layer, scatter half the rosemary, thyme and garlic. In a blender pulse the sea salt, pepper, cinnamon quill, star anise, bay leaves, lime leaves, juniper berries and sugar for 5 seconds. Rub the mixture over both sides of the duck legs and lay them over the herbs and garlic, skin side down, then sprinkle over the remaining herbs and garlic. Wrap the tray tightly with plastic wrap and refrigerate for 48 hours.

Preheat the oven to 140°C and pour the melted duck fat into a suitably deep tray. Brush the salt and herbs off the legs and lay the legs in a single layer in the tray. Cover and cook for approximately 3 hours. Remove the legs and strain the fat. Put the duck legs into a container and cover with the strained fat. Cool and store.

To serve, remove the legs carefully from the fat. Add 2 tbsp duck fat to a pan and cook the legs over a medium heat. Cook for 4–5 minutes, browning the skin well, then turn and cook for a further 3 minutes.

PORK BELLY

Preheat the oven to 150°C. Score the skin of the pork belly, rub with oil and season with salt and pepper. Mix together all remaining ingredients and pour into an oven dish. Place the pork belly on top, cover and cook for 1½ hours. Remove the cover and cook a further 30 minutes or until the meat is fork tender. Transfer the belly to a smaller tray lined with baking paper; this needs to be one-third smaller than the belly. Cover the belly with baking

Continued . . .

KUMARA FONDANTS
2 large red kumara
250 ml chicken stock
1 bunch thyme
250 g unsalted butter
salt and pepper

CHILLI AND LIME SYRUP
reserved braising liquid from
  pork belly
reserved liquid from sweet and
  sour oranges (see page 224)

sweet and sour oranges (see
  page 224)
red onion and fennel salad
  (see page 216)

paper, place another tray the same size on top with a heavy weight on top. Allow to cool in the refrigerator overnight then remove from the tray and portion. Strain the cooking liquid to use in the chilli and lime syrup.

KUMARA FONDANTS

Cut the peeled kumara into 4 cm rounds with a cookie cutter, place in a pan with the chicken stock and thyme and simmer until almost cooked, then remove from the pan. Melt the butter until foaming, add the fondants and continue cooking until golden brown. Season with salt and pepper.

CHILLI AND LIME SYRUP

Bring the reserved pork liquor to the boil and add a small amount of the orange syrup. Taste and reduce to a coating consistency.

ASSEMBLY

This dish presents well on either a large round plate or a long board. Place the duck at one end and the pork belly at the other with the fondants in the centre. Dress the components with salad and the chilli syrup and garnish with oranges.

BEST OF THE WEST

1 sprig thyme

1 tsp balsamic vinegar

1 tbsp olive oil

4 x 200 g portions venison loin

4 large Agria potatoes

salt and pepper

1 clove garlic

50 ml cream

50 g butter

¼ tsp caraway seeds

¼ red cabbage, shredded

150 ml Monteith's Celtic Red

4 rashers Blackball streaky bacon, chopped

50 ml brandy

200 ml venison glaze

Thyme-marinated venison with Monteith's Celtic Red cabbage, dauphinoise potato and brandied Blackball bacon glaze.

ACCOMPANIED WITH MONTEITH'S SINGLE SOURCE LAGER OR CELTIC RED

Strip the thyme from the stalk and chop. Combine with the balsamic vinegar and olive oil. Smother over the venison, cover and leave for at least 2 hours or overnight.

Slice the potatoes thinly, season with salt and pepper, and cook with the garlic and cream in the oven at 200°C until just soft — about 30 minutes.

Melt the butter in a heavy-bottomed saucepan, taking care not to burn it. Add the caraway seeds and shredded cabbage. When the cabbage is soft, add the beer and reduce by half. Season to taste.

Season the marinated venison and sear in a hot pan, making sure to brown all surfaces. Finish in the oven at 200°C for 8 minutes. Remove from the pan and rest for at least 5 minutes. Use the venison pan to sear the bacon, deglaze and flame with the brandy and add the venison glaze.

ASSEMBLY

Place one portion of the venison on a heated dinner plate. Place a portion of the potatoes and the cabbage on each plate. Sauce with the glaze.

WILD PORK TORTELLINI

TORTELLINI
1 tbsp fennel seeds
2 tsp chilli sambal oelek
4 cloves garlic
50 g sea salt
125 ml canola oil
300 g wild pork shoulder
fresh pasta (see page 205)
oil, for frying

CANDIED FRUIT
200 g orange marmalade
200 ml water
6 canned apricot halves,
  roughly chopped
4 canned pear halves, roughly
  chopped

ROASTED TOMATOES
4 large firm tomatoes on the
  vine
salt and pepper
olive oil

rocket leaves
blue cheese
red wine jus (see page 221)

Toasted wild pork tortellini with candied fruit, blue cheese, rocket, vine-ripened tomato, and red wine jus.

ACCOMPANIED WITH MONTEITH'S CELTIC RED

TORTELLINI
Heat the oven to 100°C. In a shallow pan lightly toast the fennel seeds, then blend in the chilli, garlic, sea salt and oil. Pierce the pork shoulder several times with a paring knife and generously smother with the marinade. Cover with tinfoil, place in the oven and cook for 8 hours. Cool and pull apart, separating out the fat and sinew. Combine with the marinade and cooking juices from the roasting pan and set aside.

Make a recipe of pasta as on page 205. Using a large cookie cutter, cut out 12 discs, working fairly quickly so the pasta does not dry out. Fill the pasta discs with the shredded pork and fold over, sealing the edges by dampening them with water and pressing them together with a fork. Fold the long edges back and press together to make the tortellini shape. Chill in the fridge until ready to plate, then deep-fry in oil. Drain on paper towels before serving.

CANDIED FRUIT
Boil the marmalade and water, add the apricot and pear, and bring to a simmer then remove from the heat.

ROASTED TOMATOES
Put the tomatoes on a tray lined with baking paper, season, add a couple of drops of olive oil and roast in the oven for 5 minutes at a high heat.

ASSEMBLY
Place the rocket, chunks of blue cheese and roasted tomato on the plate. Spoon the warmed jus around it and place the tortellini on the jus; garnish with the candied fruit.

RACK AND PINION

TAHR RACK

3 g ground fennel
salt and pepper
10 ml olive oil
4 tahr racks, silver skin
  removed, trimmed

TAHR PIE

160 g finely minced tahr meat
salt and pepper
1 g ground mace
50 ml Monteith's Celtic Red jus
  (see page 221)
250 g flour
1 tsp salt
pinch of ground fennel
90 g lard
60 ml water
milk, to glaze

SALAD

50 g cauliflower
50 g Brussels sprouts
10 g pancetta lardons or bacon
2 sprigs thyme
1 clove garlic, thinly sliced
10 g shallots
20 ml hazelnut oil
5 ml sherry vinegar
10 g toasted hazelnuts

butternut purée (see page
  208)
Monteith's Celtic Red jus (see
  page 221)

Raised tahr pie with rack of tahr on butternut purée, warm Brussels sprouts and cauliflower salad and Monteith's Celtic Red jus. Substitute goat, mutton or lamb for the tahr.

ACCOMPANIED WITH MONTEITH'S CELTIC RED

TAHR RACK

Combine the fennel, salt and pepper, and olive oil and smother over the rack. Leave to marinate for 6 hours or overnight. Heat a frying pan and brown the tahr well. Place in a 200°C oven for 8–10 minutes. Allow to rest for 10 minutes before portioning.

TAHR PIE

Combine the tahr mince, salt and pepper, mace and jus and set aside. To make the pastry, sift the flour, salt and fennel together. Heat the lard and water together in a pan until it reaches boiling point. In a mixer combine the lard and flour mix. Do not over-mix. Roll out to about 2–3 mm thick. This pastry must be used whilst it is still warm. Line four individual pie ramekins with the pastry. Place a portion of the filling (around 45 g) in each pie case and top with pastry. Cut a small hole in the tops and brush with milk. Bake at 150°C for 30–40 minutes until the liquid boils out of the hole in the top, and the pastry is golden brown.

BRUSSELS SPROUTS AND CAULIFLOWER SALAD

Cut the cauliflower into small florets. Blanch and refresh in cold water. Cut the Brussels sprouts into quarters. Blanch and refresh. Sweat the pancetta or bacon, picked thyme, garlic and shallots in the hazelnut oil. Add the sherry vinegar and reduce a little. Mix the dressing with the hazelnuts, cauliflower and Brussels sprouts. Serve warm.

ASSEMBLY

Place the pie off-centre on the plate, surround with the salad and a swipe of the purée, lean the rack across the pie and drizzle with Monteith's Celtic Red jus.

THE ORIGINAL SEABED AND BOARSHORE

CARAMELIZED PORK

1 kg wild pork belly (or
    domestic pork belly)
20 g sea salt
10 cloves
6 cloves garlic
6 star anise
2 cinnamon quills
150 g sugar

KUMARA CROQUETTES

500 g golden kumara
2 eggs
salt and pepper
1 tsp ground kawakawa
100 g breadcrumbs
150 g plain flour
60 ml milk
1 tbsp harakeke seeds
canola oil, for frying

BISQUE CREAM

60 g butter
1 crayfish head (or prawn
    heads or crab bodies/shells)
3 cloves garlic
50 g tomato paste
2 bay leaves
60 ml brandy (or white wine)
300 ml cream
salt and pepper

Caramelized wild pork with kumara, kawakawa and harakeke croquette, baked monkfish with Nelson scallop mousse and wild pork bacon, and Kaikoura crayfish bisque cream.

ACCOMPANIED WITH MONTEITH'S CRUSHED APPLE CIDER OR ORIGINAL

CARAMELIZED PORK

Preheat the oven to 150°C. Place the belly in a lined baking dish with 500 ml water. Top with sea salt, cloves, garlic, star anise and cinnamon. Cover with foil and cook in the oven until tender — about 2 hours. Allow to cool. Trim off any excess fat and dice the meat into 3 cm cubes. Add sugar to a large pan and cook carefully over a medium heat until the sugar is a caramel colour. Add the pork and stir until combined in the caramel.

KUMARA CROQUETTES

Bake the kumara whole in the oven at 180°C until soft — about 40 minutes. Cut in half and scoop out the flesh. In a bowl, mix together one egg, salt and pepper, kawakawa, and a third of the breadcrumbs. Combine with the kumara and roll into eight cylinders (depending how moist the kumara is, you may have to add more breadcrumbs). Coat each croquette in flour, then egg wash (one egg and milk) and then the remaining breadcrumbs mixed with the harakeke. To finish, fry in a deep-fryer or shallow-fry in a frying pan with canola oil till golden brown.

BISQUE CREAM

Heat the butter and crayfish, prawn or crab in a medium-sized pot over a medium heat. Crush the head with a meat mallet or similar. Add garlic, tomato paste, bay leaves and brandy or wine and combine. Add 500 ml water and simmer for 1 hour. Strain the stock into another pot, add cream and reduce till the sauce coats the back of a spoon. Season with salt and pepper to taste.

Continued . . .

MONKFISH

800 g monkfish fillets
100 g Nelson scallops (or
  imported)
1 egg
1 tbsp chives, finely chopped
60 ml cream
salt and pepper
8 rashers wild pork bacon (or
  streaky bacon)

45 ml malt vinegar

MONKFISH

Cut the monkfish into eight thin pieces of similar size, leaving 100 g for the mousse. In a food processor add the remainder of the monkfish, the scallops, egg, chives and cream and blend till smooth. Add salt and pepper to taste. Sandwich the mousse between two pieces of fish and then wrap in two rashers of bacon. Bake in the oven at 180°C for 15 minutes.

ASSEMBLY

On a plate or board place the cooked monkfish at one end and spoon warmed bisque cream over the top. At the other end place the warm caramel pork with a shot glass of malt vinegar (you can then tip as much vinegar over the pork for individual taste). In the centre of the plate place two fried croquettes, crossed.

THREE BIRDS ON A STONE

PHEASANT LEG CONFIT

1 clove garlic

5 juniper berries

4 sprigs thyme

2 sprigs rosemary

2 bay leaves

2 tsp salt

1 tsp cracked black pepper

8 pheasant legs (or chicken drums)

1½ litres duck fat (or dripping)

TERRINE

oil spray

2 tbsp karengo, fresh or dried

½ cup curly parsley, finely chopped

salt and pepper

1½ cups duck liver (or any game liver)

1 clove garlic

2 tsp chives

2 sprigs thyme

2 tsp parsley

2 tsp coriander

250 g fresh pikopiko (or asparagus)

2 pheasant breasts (or chicken breasts)

Confit of pheasant supreme, pikopiko, duck liver and pheasant breast terrine coated with a karengo and herb crust, with quail egg and smoked Cheddar soufflé seasoned with kawakawa, sauced with a trio of wild mushroom and Monteith's Celtic Red glaze, and finished with blackcurrant coulis. This recipe requires some advance preparation as the pheasant should marinate for 24 hours.

ACCOMPANIED WITH MONTEITH'S CELTIC RED

PHEASANT LEG CONFIT

Finely chop all the ingredients except for the pheasant and the duck fat to make a rub. Toss the pheasant through the rub in a bowl, cover and refrigerate for 24 hours.

Preheat the oven to 110°C. Heat the duck fat in a pan until melted. Pat the pheasant legs dry with a paper towel and place them in a single layer in a deep roasting dish. Pour the fat over so that the legs are submerged. Cover with foil, place in the oven and slowly poach for 2½ hours. The meat should be tender and fall away from the bone. Remove from the oven and lay the legs on a paper towel. Serve hot.

TERRINE

Preheat the oven to 170°C. Spray an earthenware terrine mould, with a lid, with an oil spray thoroughly. Mix together the karengo, parsley, and salt and pepper, and coat the sides of the oiled mould by rocking it back and forth until all sides are coated. Save the excess in a bowl for the top.

Dice the liver into ½ cm cubes. Chop the garlic, chives, picked thyme, parsley and coriander finely. Fold through the liver and season with salt and pepper. Press a quarter of the liver mixture into the base of the terrine mould, keeping it level. Next, place half of the pikopiko or asparagus in a layer, then another quarter of the liver mixture, pressing each layer with the palm of your hand as you go. The mould should be half full at this point. Lay

Continued . . .

GLAZE

2 bottles Monteith's Celtic Red
½ cup red cask wine
4 tsp spring onion
1 sprig thyme
2 tsp parsley
pepper
1 tbsp redcurrant jelly
2 tsp arrowroot (or cornflour)
2 tbsp brown sugar
3 portobello mushrooms
5 shiitake mushrooms
10 clamshell mushrooms

QUAIL EGG SOUFFLÉ

oil spray
12 quail egg whites
4 chicken egg whites
8 tsp smoked Cheddar
4 tsp ground kawakawa
8 quail egg yolks
salt and pepper

blackcurrant coulis (see
  page 225)

the two pheasant breasts down the centre of the mould; this way they can be seen right through the centre when the terrine is cut. Cover with another quarter of the liver mixture, pressing it down tight and level. Follow with the remaining pikopiko, then the remaining quarter of the liver. Sprinkle the last of the karengo mixture over the top and place the lid on.

Bake in the oven in a water bath for 1¼ hours or until the core temperature has reached 70–80°C. A roasting dish is ideal for a water bath. Remove from the oven and stand for 15 minutes, then turn onto a rack. Cool before slicing, and serve cold.

MONTEITH'S CELTIC RED GLAZE

Reduce the beer and wine by half by boiling together in a saucepan. Finely chop the spring onion, picked thyme and parsley and add to the liquor with pepper and redcurrant jelly. Thicken slightly by slowly adding the arrowroot or cornflour dissolved in water, whisking to a glaze. Add sugar little by little to taste, making sure it's not too sweet. Chop the mushrooms and add to the sauce. Cook until the mushrooms are soft.

QUAIL EGG SOUFFLÉ

Preheat the oven to 190–200°C (on conventional bake). Grease the sides of four small ramekins with an oil spray. The sides of the ramekins can be heightened by taping baking paper around the sides. This will avoid overflowing and the soufflé will rise upwards. If paper is added, the inner sides will need to be greased to avoid sticking.

When separating the eggs, no egg yolk should be in the whites. Whisk the egg whites in a large bowl to stiff peaks. Grate the Cheddar, add the kawakawa, and mix with the egg yolks and seasoning. Fold the stiff egg whites into the yolk mixture with a spatula, being careful not to lose any air from the whites. Once combined, spoon into the ramekins and bake in the oven for 20 minutes. Remove the paper before serving. The soufflés must be served immediately otherwise they will sink.

ASSEMBLY

Place a slice of cold terrine onto the plate. Lean the two pheasant legs together, hot and drained from the confit. Drizzle the coulis around the plate and spoon Monteith's Celtic Red glaze over the pheasant. Place the soufflé behind the pheasant and the terrine. Garnish with a stem of pikopiko or asparagus and serve immediately.

WILD VENISON LOIN

1 kg venison loin (Raukumara Red)

150 g chicken breast

1 egg

100 ml cream

zest of 1 orange

1 bunch thyme, chopped

salt and pepper

10 pieces wild boar bacon

2 large Agria potatoes

12 baby carrots

6 baby turnips

6 golden baby beetroot

100 g raisins

80 ml brandy

40 ml canola oil

150 g shallots, finely sliced

1 chicken or duck frame, chopped

100 ml port wine

600 ml chicken stock

40 ml beef stock

4 egg whites

baby chard, to garnish

Wild venison loin wrapped in wild boar bacon with an autumn vegetable medley and brandy raisins, finished with game consommé.

ACCOMPANIED WITH MONTEITH'S RADLER

Trim the venison loin. Take 150 g of the venison and place the rest of the loin in the fridge for later. Place the chicken breast and venison in a food processor, pulse until combined, add the egg and cream and process until it is all well combined. This will be your stuffing or farce. Pass the farce through a drum sieve to get rid of any leftover bits of sinew. Add orange zest, picked thyme (saving a couple of sprigs) and seasoning. Mix well and place in the fridge.

Roll out a piece of plastic wrap on the kitchen bench and lay the bacon pieces down, making sure they are overlapping each other by about ½ cm. Spread a layer of the farce over the bacon, making sure you cover all the bacon with an even layer. Remove the remaining loin from the fridge, season with salt and pepper and place on the edge of the bacon and farce. Gently pick up the plastic wrap and roll the loin so the bacon wraps around the loin, then roll the wrapped loin so it tightens up a little. Tie the ends of the plastic wrap and place in the freezer for 20 minutes.

Remove from the freezer and cut into four 200 g portions. Repeat the plastic wrap process again so you end up with four portions of wrapped loin. Place the portions in a water bath (heated to 59°C) for 1 hour.

Dice the potatoes into cubes, then parboil in salted water for 6 minutes. Remove from the water straight into ice water. Place the baby carrots into boiling water for 4 minutes, remove and place into an ice bath. With the baby turnips and beetroot, place in boiling water for 8 minutes or until the skins are ready to fall off. Once this is happening, remove them from the water and place into an ice bath. The skins should be able to be rubbed off. Halve the turnips and beetroot, then place all the vegetables into a bowl and set aside.

Continued . . .

Put the raisins in a pan with the brandy and place on the stove top over a low heat for about 10 minutes or until the raisins have soaked up all the brandy. Remove from the pan and set aside.

Heat a large pot with the canola oil over a high heat for 3–4 minutes. Add the shallots and cook until golden brown. Meanwhile, place the chicken or duck bones in a hot 180°C oven for 30 minutes to brown. Add the remaining thyme to the shallots, cook out until fragrant, and add the wine. Lower the heat to medium, and reduce by half. Add the roasted bones and both stocks to the pot and reduce by half. Strain into another pot, removing all of the bones, shallots and thyme, and skim off the excess fat. Bring the sauce back up to a simmer. Whisk the egg whites until they have doubled in size, add them to the sauce and stir until the white comes to the top (this is the raft). Strain the consommé through two filters and discard the white to the bin. Taste the consommé and season if required.

Remove the loins from the water bath, remove the plastic wrap, and season with salt and pepper. Heat a pan with a little oil, and seal the loins until the bacon is golden brown. Remove from the pan and rest for 5 minutes, keeping them warm. In a medium pot heat the consommé until simmering, add the vegetables and heat through (4–6 minutes), then add the soaked raisins.

ASSEMBLY

Slice the venison loin into three pieces and place in the centre of a plate. Arrange the vegetables and raisins around the loin, and pour over the consommé. Garnish with baby chard.

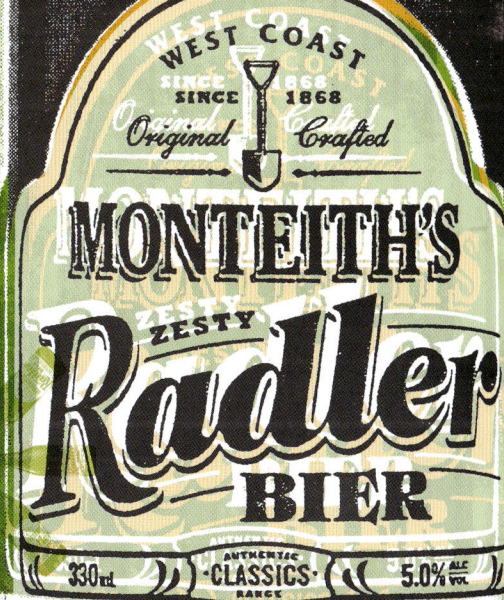

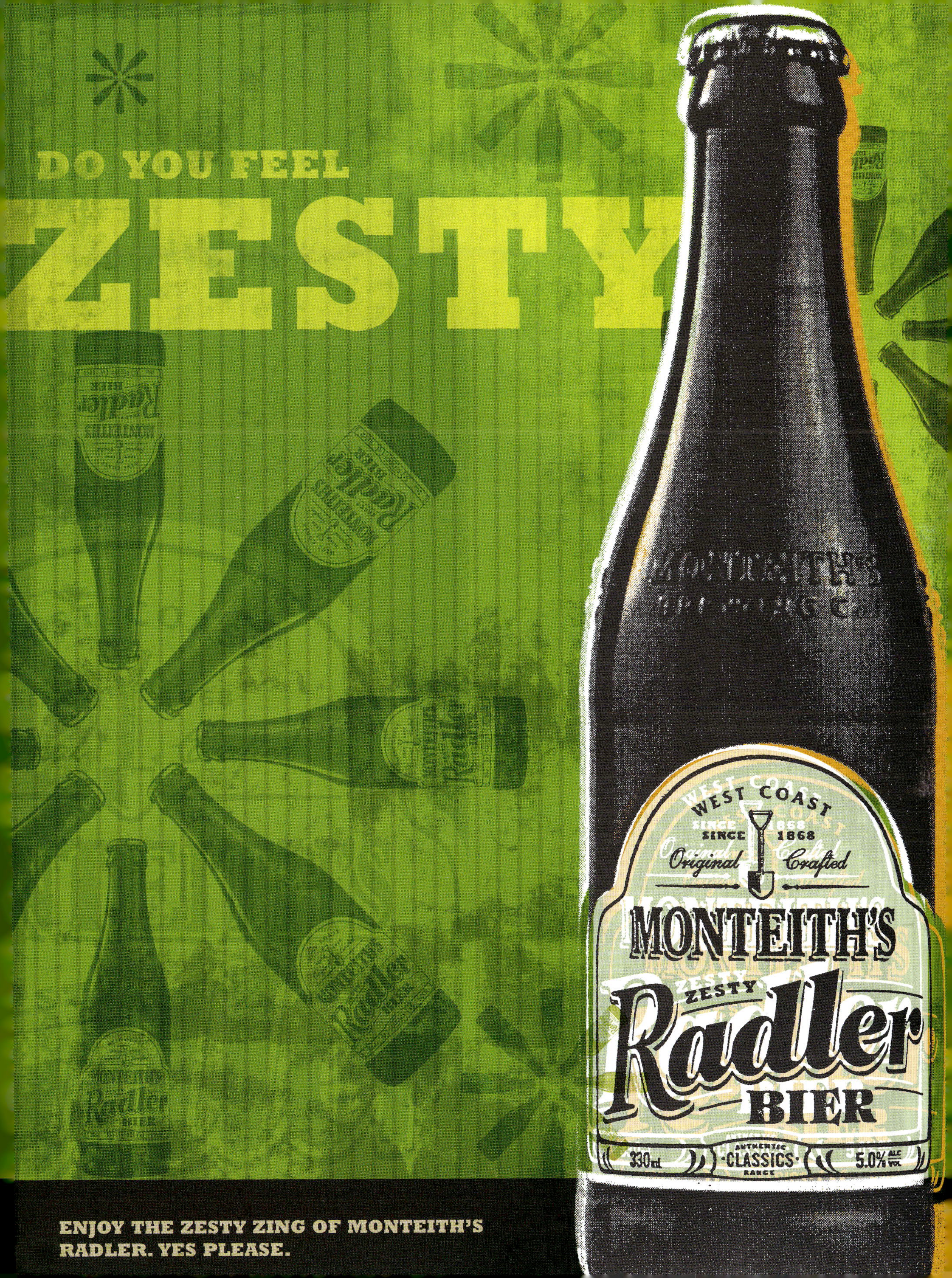
DO YOU FEEL
ZESTY
WEST COAST
SINCE 1868
Original Crafted
MONTEITH'S
ZESTY
Radler
BIER
330ml
AUTHENTIC
CLASSICS
RANGE
5.0% ALC VOL
ENJOY THE ZESTY ZING OF MONTEITH'S RADLER. YES PLEASE.

MAKE ME WILD, YOUNG SNAPPER

1 tsp olive oil

4 x 200 g snapper fillets
(or any firm white fish, e.g.
gurnard, monkfish or groper)

sea salt

freshly ground black pepper

1 fennel bulb, thinly sliced,
keeping fronds for garnish

150 ml white wine

350 ml cream

2 cloves garlic, crushed

½ cup caramelized shallots
(see page 205)

170 g sun-dried tomatoes (or
85 g semi-dried tomatoes)

80 g spring onion, sliced

chopped coriander, to taste

4 cooked new potatoes,
crushed

1 bunch watercress

1 roasted red capsicum, sliced

70 g pine nuts, toasted

Snapper with fennel, toasted pine nuts, sun-dried tomatoes and caramelized shallot poaching sauce.

ACCOMPANIED WITH MONTEITH'S RADLER

Heat the olive oil in a large frying pan. Season the fleshy side of the snapper fillets with salt and pepper. Lay the fillets in the pan, seasoned side down, and allow to brown. Add the sliced fennel and brown. Turn the fillets, then add the wine, cream, garlic, caramelized shallots and tomatoes. Reduce the sauce until the cream starts to take on a yellow tinge. Remove the pan from the heat and add the spring onion and chopped coriander leaf. Check the seasoning and adjust if required.

ASSEMBLY

Place the crushed potato on a warmed plate. Place the fish fillets on the potato and baste with the sauce. Serve with fresh watercress, roasted red capsicum and fennel fronds. Garnish with toasted pine nuts.

'LOOK HARE,' A WILD LITTLE PIG SAID, 'SO WHAT IF I'M WITH A TART!'

WILD HARE RAGOUT
200 g wild pork fat lardons
10 ml olive oil
50 g wild thyme
1½ litres beef stock reduction
2 kg wild hare bones
1 bouquet garni
1 kg hare, diced
1 large white onion, diced
1 large carrot, diced
1 stick celery, diced
1 roasted red capsicum,
  skinned and diced
50 ml brandy
50 ml port
salt and pepper

PERUPERU AND PIKOPIKO
500 g peruperu potatoes
12 pikopiko fronds
butter

CARAMELIZED SHALLOT TART
200 g shallots, peeled and
  blanched
20 g butter
10 g thyme
2 sheets flaky puff pastry
1 egg yolk
ground horopito

BRAISED WILD PORK BELLY
1 kg wild pork belly
50 g 13 spice mix
1 litre pineapple juice

Wild hare ragout and pork belly, horopito, thyme and caramelized shallot tart, pikopiko and Maori potato.

ACCOMPANIED WITH MONTEITH'S ORIGINAL

WILD HARE RAGOUT
Render the pork fat and olive oil together with the thyme. Remove the thyme and place in a pot with the stock, hare bones and bouquet garni. Heat the stock mixture. Brown the wild hare meat in the rendered fat. You will need to do this in stages. Once the hare is browned, add the diced vegetables and lightly brown. Deglaze the pan with the brandy and port. Strain the hot stock and add to the hare and vegetables. Bring to the boil, then simmer for 3 hours or until tender. Once tender, adjust the seasoning with sea salt and cracked black pepper.

PERUPERU AND PIKOPIKO
Bring the potatoes to the boil and cook until tender. Once cooked, cool slightly and peel. Bring some water to the boil, blanch and refresh the pikopiko for 10 seconds and then toss with the potatoes and a knob of butter.

CARAMELIZED SHALLOT TART
Slowly caramelize the shallots in butter with picked thyme, and adjust the seasoning. Cool. Cut out desired shapes of pastry, place onto a greased baking tray, brush with egg yolk and dust with horopito. Bake at 190°C until golden brown. Remove from the oven and cut through the middle so you have a top and bottom. Spoon caramelized onion into the pastry.

BRAISED WILD PORK BELLY
Braise the pork for at least 3 hours in the spices and pineapple juice. Cool and press with a heavy weight to flatten. Cut into 1 cm thick lengths. Reheat as required.

Continued . . .

ASSEMBLY
Place a portion of the wild hare ragout onto a heated plate and scatter the vegetables over. Top with a slice of pork belly. Garnish with a frond of fresh pikopiko and serve with a shallot tart.

KINK IN MY NECK

BRAISED LAMB NECK
2 lamb necks (boneless)
½ carrot, chopped
½ white onion, chopped
1 head garlic, skin on
1 cup white wine
100 g peas (can be frozen)
½ bunch pea shoots

ROASTED BABY BEETROOT
16 baby beetroot
100 ml balsamic vinegar
50 g brown sugar
2 tbsp olive oil
1 tsp freshly ground coffee

JUS
200 ml reduced braising liquid
100 ml Pinot Noir
70 g port wine jelly

potato dauphine (see page 211)
cauliflower and Persian purée
  (see page 211)
garlic confit (see page 208)
micro greens

Slow-braised Manawatu lamb neck served with roasted cauliflower and Persian purée, potato and feta puffs, garlic confit, balsamic baby beets and a jus reduction.

ACCOMPANIED WITH MONTEITH'S CELTIC RED OR PILSNER

BRAISED LAMB NECK
Preheat the oven to 120°C. Braise the lamb neck with the carrot, onion, garlic and white wine, adding enough water to cover, for approximately 3 hours or until soft. Reserve half of the braising liquid for next time you braise, and reduce the remaining half to finish the plate. When the lamb is tender, press it between two trays. Roast the pressed meat in a roasting dish with the peas at 200°C for 6 minutes, until the lamb is crispy and the peas are cooked, then fold through the pea shoots.

BALSAMIC ROASTED BABY BEETROOT
Cut the stalks of the beets to 20 mm. Place all the ingredients in an ovenproof dish and bake at 180°C for 40 minutes.

JUS
Combine all ingredients in a saucepan and reduce until it becomes a thin syrup.

ASSEMBLY
Place a square of potato dauphine in the centre of the plate. Spoon jus around the plate. Place a tablespoon of purée next to the potato, and top with the lamb. Add the peas, garlic confit and beetroot. Garnish with micro greens.

VENISON, SWEETIE?

750 ml red wine

2 cinnamon quills

zest of 1 lemon

pinch of ground cloves

4 small firm pears, peeled

300 g sugar

4 x 200 g venison tenderloins

salt and pepper

50 g butter, plus extra

4 parsnips

4 carrots

100 ml red wine jus (see page 221)

100 g red kumara

oil, for frying

Venison medallions with crushed root vegetables and kumara crisps.

ACCOMPANIED WITH MONTEITH'S BLACK

Place the red wine in a large saucepan and bring to a simmer. Add the cinnamon, lemon zest and ground cloves and simmer for 5 minutes. Add the whole pears and sugar. Partly cover and simmer over a very low heat for 1 hour until the pears are tender. Carefully remove the pears with a slotted spoon and place in a heatproof serving dish. Strain the remaining red wine mixture and return to the saucepan. Bring to the boil and cook briskly until it reduces and thickens into a syrup.

Place the seasoned venison into a hot pan with the butter. Seal every surface of the meat until a rich brown colour. Place the venison in a preheated 180°C oven for 10 minutes, then rest in a warm place.

Roughly chop the parsnips and carrots and cook in boiling water until soft, then drain. Mash the carrot and parsnip, then add a little butter and seasoning. Place the pear syrup in a saucepan, add the red wine jus and reduce until thickened. Add seasoning and a touch of butter for taste. Thinly slice the kumara and deep-fry until golden brown.

ASSEMBLY

Place a generous spoonful of carrot and parsnip mash on a heated plate. Rest the meat on top and pour over the jus. Serve with a hot pear and kumara crisps.

SLOW GOAT TO ARROWTOWN

5 cloves garlic, finely chopped

7 g rosemary, chopped

30 g fresh red chilli, sliced

salt and pepper

70 ml lime juice

180 ml extra virgin olive oil

2 kg goat shoulder chops, trimmed (or 6–7 lamb cutlets)

180 g shallots, sliced

300 g seeded tomatoes, chopped into quarters

1 x 350 g can butter beans in brine

700 g baby potatoes, skin on, cut into 2 cm cubes

400 g carrots, chopped

3 bottles Monteith's Celtic Red

1 red cabbage, chopped into 4 pieces

10 g coriander, chopped

20 g Italian parsley, chopped

30 g spring onion, chopped

steamed rice or kumara mash, to serve

Monteith's Celtic Red slow-cooked goat shoulder stew. Marinate the chops overnight for best results.

ACCOMPANIED WITH MONTEITH'S RADLER

Combine the garlic, rosemary, chilli, salt and pepper, lime juice and olive oil (saving 50 ml) and rub into the chops. Place the chops into a large container, seal and leave to rest overnight.

The next day place 50 ml olive oil in a pan and sauté the shallots. Add the marinated chops and sauté until golden. Add the tomatoes and cook for 3 minutes, then add the butter beans, potatoes and carrots. Cover with Monteith's Celtic Red. Bring to the boil and cook for 5 minutes over a high heat. Reduce the heat to medium and with the lid on simmer for 1¼ hours, checking the beer level and adding more if required to keep the meat covered.

After 45 minutes add the four pieces of red cabbage one by one, leaving them in complete pieces on top of the meat. After 1 hour and 10 minutes add the coriander, Italian parsley and spring onion. Cook for a further 5 minutes and serve.

ASSEMBLY

Serve hot in deep bowls with steamed rice or kumara mash.

Beer and food matching

◄ **HONEY, THE DUCK'S SWEET ON THE SOW!**
with
MONTEITH'S RADLER

► **BEST OF THE WEST**
with
MONTEITH'S SINGLE SOURCE LAGER

◄ **WILD PORK TORTELLINI**
with
MONTEITH'S CELTIC RED

► **RACK AND PINION**
with
MONTEITH'S CELTIC RED

◄ **THE ORIGINAL SEABED AND BOARSHORE**
with
MONTEITH'S CRUSHED APPLE CIDER

► **THREE BIRDS ON A STONE**
with
MONTEITH'S CELTIC RED

◄

WILD VENISON LOIN
with
MONTEITH'S RADLER

―――――――――

►

**MAKE ME WILD, YOUNG
SNAPPER**
with
MONTEITH'S RADLER

―――――――――

◄

**'LOOK HARE,' A WILD LITTLE
PIG SAID, 'SO WHAT IF I'M
WITH A TART!'**
with
MONTEITH'S ORIGINAL

―――――――――

►

KINK IN MY NECK
with
MONTEITH'S CELTIC RED

―――――――――

◄

VENISON, SWEETIE?
with
MONTEITH'S BLACK

―――――――――

►

SLOW GOAT TO ARROWTOWN
with
MONTEITH'S RADLER

―――――――――

WILD PETER RABBIT

300 g carrots, cut into 2 cm cubes

300 g celery, cut into 2 cm cubes

500 g onions, roughly diced

2 medium-sized wild rabbits, separated into frames, loin, forelegs and hind legs

900 ml Monteith's Black

4 bay leaves

10 black peppercorns

5 cloves garlic

50 g tomato paste

salt and pepper

80 g prunes, sliced thinly

150 g dry-cured bacon

600 g carrots

50 g butter

pinch of nutmeg

white pepper

800 g red kumara, diced

1 tbsp honey

400 g silver beet, shredded

1 white onion, thinly sliced

A succulent roast of braised rabbit with all the trimmings.

ACCOMPANIED WITH MONTEITH'S PILSNER

Preheat the oven to 200°C. Roast the carrots, celery, onions and rabbit frames in a large deep roasting tray till golden brown (approximately 30–40 minutes). Add the beer, bay leaves, peppercorns, garlic, forelegs and hind legs. Place baking paper over the dish then seal with tinfoil. Cook at 150°C for 3 hours or until the meat is tender. Remove the hind and forelegs and set aside. Reserve the roasting tray ingredients.

Add 1 litre water to the roasting tray and reserved ingredients, stir and pass all solid ingredients through a sieve. Add tomato paste and reduce the liquid until it has thickened to the desired consistency. Taste and adjust the seasoning.

Butterfly the loin, adding prunes along the middle, fold the loin over and roll the bacon tightly around the outside. Place in a hot ovenproof pan with a small amount of oil and bake at 200°C for 3–4 minutes. Remove from the oven and rest for a further 2 minutes.

Slice the carrots thinly, add the butter and nutmeg and season with salt and white pepper. Cook on a very low heat for 10–15 minutes, covered, until the carrot is very tender. Process in a blender or with a stick blender until completely smooth. Taste and adjust the seasoning. Toss the kumara with the honey and roast till golden brown, then season. Pull the meat off the rabbit forelegs and stir into the silver beet and onion. Sauté until tender and season with salt and pepper.

ASSEMBLY

Place a generous portion of carrot purée onto the plate. Place the roasted kumara to the side and rest the hind legs on top. Slice the loin and rest on the silver beet and rabbit mix. Cover the hind legs with sauce and serve.

TASTE OF SOUTHERN SEAS

500 g snapper fillets, skin and
   bones removed
1 young coconut
juice of 4 limes
sea salt
1 bunch fresh coriander,
   chopped
1 tbsp chives, finely chopped
3 tbsp extra virgin olive oil
3 red radishes
1 telegraph cucumber
1 spring onion

Ceviche of snapper and young coconut.

ACCOMPANIED WITH MONTEITH'S RADLER

Slice the snapper as thinly as possible in the style of sashimi. Split the young coconut in half, retaining the juice. Using a tablespoon, scoop out the coconut flesh and slice into roughly the same size pieces as the fish. Add the lime juice to the fish with enough sea salt to taste. Add the coconut flesh, coriander, chives, olive oil and 150 ml of the coconut juice. Set aside to marinate for 15 minutes.

While the fish is marinating, slice the radishes into paper-thin slices and place in iced water to make them nice and crunchy. Peel the cucumber, cut lengthwise and scoop out the seeds. Dice into small cubes and add to the fish mixture. Finely chop the spring onion, discarding the dark green ends, then add to the fish mix. By now the fish will have gone slightly translucent, meaning the acid from the lime and salt has penetrated the flesh and has gently cured the fish so it's ready to serve.

ASSEMBLY
Place the fish in a serving bowl, adding the sliced radish in stages for presentation. Garnish with coriander and a few extra lime wedges.

FOUR WILD PIGS IN THE ORCHARD

WILD PORK TENDERLOIN

1 kg wild pork tenderloin

150 g streaky bacon, sliced about 2 mm thick and 22 cm long

250 g wild pork mousse (see page 212)

1 tbsp flaky sea salt

½ tsp cracked white pepper

4 tbsp thyme, chopped

zest of 2 lemons

WILD BOAR CIGAR

150 g wild boar ragout (see page 129)

3 sheets filo pastry, stacked and cut into 6 squares

100 g butter, melted

Bacon-wrapped wild pork tenderloin with a filo cigar of wild boar neck, wild pork tortellini, roasted fruit, nuts and root vegetables, Granny Smith apple sauce, Madeira jus and wild watercress. Don't be put off by the complexity of this dish. Following the steps in sequence will result in a truly fabulous meal, well worth the effort.

ACCOMPANIED WITH MONTEITH'S CRUSHED APPLE CIDER

WILD PORK TENDERLOIN

Use a sharp knife to trim off the first 3 cm of the thin end of the tenderloins and about the same off the thick end. Carefully remove the silver skin and excess fat. Set all of the trim aside to make your mousse; you should have about 750 g of tenderloin and about 250 g of trim. Lay the chilled bacon slices side by side on a 30 cm x 44 cm piece of baking paper. Spread the mousse over the full width and three-quarters of the length of the bacon sheet, then evenly season with salt and pepper, picked thyme and lemon zest. Evenly divide the tenderloin across the width of the bacon sheet, season the meat with a little more sea salt and roll firmly to form a large sausage-like cylinder. Wrap the cylinder in plastic wrap and twist until tight, then tie off the ends and allow to set for at least 2–4 hours or overnight.

Once the wild pork has set, unwrap it and use a sharp knife to cut it into six even portions. Vacuum-pack each portion individually and set aside in the fridge until needed. They will keep for 4–5 days vacuum-packed and refrigerated. If you do not have access to a vacuum-packer, just wrap them in plastic wrap and cook within 2–3 days.

WILD BOAR CIGAR

Put the wild pork ragout into a heavy-bottomed saucepan, gently bring it to a simmer and cook until most of the liquid has evaporated. Spread the ragout onto a small tray and cool in the fridge. Lay all six filo squares side by side and brush generously

Continued . . .

WILD PORK TORTELLINI

150 g wild pork mousse (see page 212)

zest of ½ orange

2 tbsp chives, chopped

2 tbsp toasted walnuts, chopped

fresh pasta (see page 205)

FRUIT, NUTS AND VEGETABLES

18 large seedless grapes

2 Granny Smith apples, cored

2 ripe pears, cored

2 fennel bulbs

juice of 1 lemon

18 baby carrots

12 roasted chestnuts (canned)

roasted shallots (see page 207)

COOKING

flaky sea salt

olive oil

canola or grapeseed oil

150 g unsalted butter

2 cloves garlic, skin on, crushed

2 sprigs thyme

Madeira jus (see page 222)

1 shallot, diced very finely

2 tbsp chives, chopped very finely

Granny Smith apple sauce (see page 216)

wild watercress

with the melted butter. Evenly divide the boar six ways and place a cigar-shaped portion onto the centre of each pastry square, then roll up and twist the ends. Brush with butter and store in the fridge for up to a week.

WILD PORK TORTELLINI

Fold all of the ingredients except the pasta together with a rubber spatula, and set aside. Divide the farce into 12 even-sized balls and set aside. Flatten the pasta with a rolling pin until it is thin enough to put through the thickest setting of the pasta machine and roll it through twice, then fold it in half and repeat until the pasta is as wide as the width of the machine and very smooth. Dust on both sides with a little fine semolina and run through the settings until you have reached the thinnest one. Dust the work surface with a little more semolina and carefully lay the very thin pasta sheet down, being sure not to fold the ends as they may stick together.

Use a 10 cm diameter round cookie cutter to cut out 12 circles of pasta, then very lightly spray them with a mist of water. Place a wild pork ball onto the centre of each pasta round and fold them in half to form a half-circle, making sure to press the pasta around the ball, removing all of the air. Twist the two pointed corners around your thumb and bring them together to meet at the centre of the ball, and press the two ends together. They should stand by themselves and look like a round wonton.

Place your tortellini on a shallow bed of semolina and dust a little more on top and refrigerate until needed. This dish only requires one tortellini per portion, so store the extras in the fridge for one day or freeze them for up to a month.

FRUIT, NUTS AND VEGETABLES

Peel the grapes and cut the apple, pear and fennel into eighths. As you work, place them into iced water and lemon juice to prevent them from turning brown. Trim the green leaf of the baby carrots, peel and clean around the green stalk. Cook the fennel and the baby carrots in boiling salted water for about 5 minutes until just tender, then quickly cool in iced water. The chestnuts and shallots are ready to use as is.

COOKING

Preheat the oven to 220°C. Fill a medium-sized saucepan with cold water, add enough flaky sea salt until you can just taste it

Continued . . .

and a splash of olive oil. Bring it to the boil ready to cook the tortellini.

Use a heavy-bottomed ovenproof frying pan big enough to fit all six pork tenderloin portions. Bring it to a medium–high heat, add a couple of tablespoons of oil, then caramelize all sides of the meat. Keep turning the pork until golden all the way round, then flip them onto the flat side and place the pan into the oven. After about 6–8 minutes flip them onto the other flat side and cook for a further 8 minutes or longer, to taste. Put the pan back on the element, flip the wild pork back onto the bacon side, add a couple of big tablespoons of butter, the garlic and thyme, and allow the heat to foam the butter. Spoon this wonderfully scented foam over the pork portions for a minute, then remove from the heat to rest for about 5 minutes. They will feel quite soft.

For the filo cigars, place a piece of baking paper on a small ovenproof tray, evenly space the cigars on the paper and put them in the oven when you flip the wild pork onto the second flat side. The cigars will take about 10 minutes to become golden and crispy.

Use at least a 26 cm diameter deep ovenproof frying pan to cook the roasted fruit, nuts and vegetables. As soon as the filo cigars go into the oven, heat the pan on medium–high and add a couple of tablespoons of oil. Dry the apple and pear and allow them to lightly caramelize before adding the fennel and baby carrots. Allow them to caramelize too, then add the roasted shallots and chestnuts. Season lightly with flaky sea salt and cracked white pepper, then place in the oven to roast for 4–5 minutes. When you pull the pan out of the oven, add about 200 ml of the Madeira jus and bring to the boil. Add the remaining 100 g or so of butter and let it simmer until the sauce becomes shiny and glazes all of the ingredients. Add the grapes, chopped shallots and chives. Adjust the seasoning with salt and pepper, if needed.

Drop the tortellini into simmering water and cook for 4 minutes until the pasta is tender, then add to the pan of fruit, nuts and vegetables and fold through the sauce.

ASSEMBLY
Divide the tortellini, glazed goodies and sauce between four heated dinner plates. Slice each wild pork roll into three and place them on the plate, then add the filo cigars, a spoon of cold apple sauce and finish with wild watercress.

WILD BOAR RAGOUT

2½ kg wild boar necks
  (boneless)
2 tbsp flaky sea salt
1 tbsp oil
2 large fennel bulbs, sliced
2 large yellow onions, chopped
½ tbsp fennel seeds, lightly
  toasted
½ tbsp coriander seeds, lightly
  toasted
½ tbsp white peppercorns
1 cup tomato fondue (see
  page 219, or ½ can crushed
  tomatoes)
2 cups Prosecco (or any sweet
  sparkling wine)

PAPPARDELLE
300 g strong flour
100 g fine semolina (or strong
  flour)
8 egg yolks
2 whole eggs

shaved pecorino
chives

Wild boar ragout with fresh pappardelle, pecorino and chives.

ACCOMPANIED WITH MONTEITH'S SINGLE SOURCE LAGER

Dry the blood off the boar necks and season them well with sea salt. Caramelize in a pan with the oil to a dark golden colour and place them in a large roasting dish. Caramelize the vegetables, add the spices, the tomato fondue or crushed tomatoes and the Prosecco, then bring it all to the boil and pour it over the boar meat. The boar should be three-quarters covered with liquid; if it isn't, just top up the roasting pan with water or chicken stock. Cover the roasting pan with foil and braise at 150°C until the meat is very tender. This will take approximately 4–5 hours. When the meat is very tender, carefully separate it from the braising liquor, break it up into bite-size chunks and set them aside.

Purée the vegetables and liquids in a blender until it is a smooth silky sauce, then fold the meat back into the sauce. Adjust the seasoning, if needed.

PAPPARDELLE
Mix the flour and semolina together on a clean surface. Make a well in the centre and add the egg yolks. Mix with a fork, bringing the flour to the middle until you have enough of a dough to mix by hand. Knead well until a smooth, elastic dough forms. If the dough is too sticky add more flour, or if it is too dry add more egg. Wrap in plastic wrap and rest in the fridge for 30 minutes. Remove from the fridge and cut into four pieces. Work with one at a time; keep the others covered.

Flatten the pasta with a rolling pin until it is thin enough to put through the thickest setting of the pasta machine, then fold it in half and repeat a couple of times until the pasta is as wide as the width of the machine and very smooth. Dust the pasta on both sides with a little fine semolina and run it through the settings until you have reached the desired thickness, about

Continued . . .

2 mm. Cut the pasta sheets into lengths of about 20 cm, dust them with fine semolina and roll them into tubes, then cut into ribbons about 4 cm wide. When you are ready to use the pappardelle, unroll them and drop them into a pot of lightly salted boiling water and cook for about 3–4 minutes until they are just tender.

Note: Your pappardelle will stay fresh in the fridge for about half a day, then you can dry any left over by hanging it over a coat hanger for a couple of days in a dry place until you can crumble it in your hand. Store it in an airtight container for up to two months.

ASSEMBLY
Toss the pappardelle in soft butter and divide between eight plates. Spoon the wild boar ragout over and finish with freshly shaved pecorino cheese and chives.

SMOKED FISH PIE

SMOKED FISH

½ cinnamon quill

1 star anise

¼ tbsp coriander seeds

¼ tbsp fennel seeds

½ cup sea salt

½ cup soft brown sugar

500 g firm white fish fillets, skin on (e.g. snapper, warehou)

100 g manuka bark or wood chips

PIE FILLING

2 cups fish velouté (see page 221)

50 g unsalted butter

1 carrot, diced

1 small onion, diced

1 small stick celery, diced

4 sprigs thyme, finely chopped

1 small bay leaf (fresh or dry)

½ cup dry white wine

½ tbsp sea salt

6 boiled eggs, cut into quarters

½ cup curly parsley, chopped

This recipe is inspired by my dad's smoked fish pie that I remember so fondly from my childhood.

ACCOMPANIED WITH MONTEITH'S SINGLE SOURCE LAGER

TO SMOKE FISH

Lightly toast the spices separately in a frying pan, then add to the salt and grind into a powder using a mortar and pestle or a spice grinder. Add the sugar and mix well. Generously smother the flesh of the fish fillets with the spice mix and refrigerate for 3 hours. Rinse the fish off in water, pat dry and set aside.

Line a deep baking dish with foil, add the bark, fit an appropriate-sized cake rack inside the dish, then lay the fish on top, skin side down. Heat over an open flame (or electric is fine) until the bark begins to smoke, then lower the heat, cover the dish with foil and smoke for about 10 minutes. Cool without removing the foil. The fish should be firm but still moist. Once cool, remove the skin and bones and break the fish into bite-size pieces, then set aside.

PIE FILLING

While the velouté is cooking, prepare the ingredients for the filling. Melt the butter in a deep saucepan and lightly fry the vegetables until they appear opaque. Add the picked thyme and bay leaf and gently cook with a tight lid on for 5 minutes. Add the wine and salt and reduce by three-quarters, then add the velouté to the vegetable stew and cook slowly to form a thick sauce. This may take only 5 minutes. Fold through the smoked fish, boiled eggs and parsley, adjusting the seasoning if you think it needs it. Pour the pie filling into an appropriate-sized baking dish and allow to cool to room temperature; this will make it easier to add the topping.

Continued . . .

POTATO TOPPING

1½ kg Agria potatoes (or any mashing potato), peeled and diced
salt and pepper
4 egg yolks
75 g butter
pinch of fresh grated nutmeg
1 whole egg, to glaze

POTATO TOPPING

Place the potatoes in cold salted water, bring to the boil, then simmer gently until tender, about 20 minutes. Drain off the water and dry the potatoes out over the heat, then pass them through a sieve or potato ricer. Add the remaining ingredients except for the whole egg and mix well with a spatula over a medium heat. Use a wooden spatula to spread the potato topping over the fish mixture. Beat the egg and brush on the topping to achieve an even glossy coating. Season with salt and pepper and bake at 200°C until golden.

ASSEMBLY

Serve a generous slice of the pie with grilled bread and a light green salad.

Note: If you have any leftover potato, try making your own potato puffs. Roll the potato into small balls, dip them in beaten egg and bake until golden.

XTREME GAME

200 g minced paua
salt and pepper
2 tbsp breadcrumbs
1 spring onion, sliced
1 kg wild venison Denver leg
  (or farmed venison)
8 long strips streaky bacon
200 ml packet European
  Gourmet jus or demi-
  glaze (available from most
  supermarkets)
olive oil
12 gourmet potatoes, boiled
  and cut into wedges
200 g chorizo, sliced
120 g baby spinach, washed
  and dried
fresh paua, to serve

Venison with paua stuffing and chorizo on potato wedges.

ACCOMPANIED WITH MONTEITH'S CELTIC RED

In a bowl combine paua, salt and pepper, breadcrumbs and spring onion. Mix well as if making a stuffing. Clean off all the silver skin on the Denver leg and cut into four even-sized portions. Lay the portions on a chopping board and make pockets in the venison so they are across the grain of the meat. Stuff the venison with the paua mince. Lay two bacon strips on the chopping board. Place a venison portion on top of the bacon and fold the bacon over the pocket. Overlap the bacon and use two toothpicks to secure the bacon in place. Repeat this with each venison portion, cover, and place in the fridge until needed.

Preheat the oven to 210°C. Heat the jus or demi-glaze in a saucepan. At the same time place a non-stick pan on the heat. Once the pan is hot, add a little olive oil and sear all the surfaces of the venison until golden brown. Remove from the heat and place on an oven tray. Place in the hot oven for 8 minutes.

About a minute before the venison comes out of the oven, heat a large pan and sauté the gourmet potatoes until nicely coloured. Remove the venison from the oven and rest. In the pan combine the sliced chorizo with the gourmet potatoes and colour before adding the spinach. Cook until the spinach is lightly wilted. Season with salt and remove from the heat.

ASSEMBLY
Preheat four dinner plates. Place even portions of the potato and spinach on each plate. Slice the venison across the grain and place to one side. Drizzle with the jus, garnish with slices of fresh paua and serve.

PIE, DEER?

PIE FILLING

1 tbsp ground kawakawa

1 juniper berry, crushed

800 g venison (preferably shoulder or neck), cubed

seasoned flour

4 tbsp olive oil

1 clove garlic, crushed

200 ml red wine

400 ml beef or venison stock

10 g bitter chocolate

SMOKED EEL HASH

4 large potatoes (preferably Agria), peeled

salt and white pepper

150 ml cream

2 tbsp butter

50 g smoked eel (or any smoked fish)

PASTRY CASE

oil or butter, for greasing

savoury pastry, cut into strips approx 2½ cm wide and 30 cm long

1 egg, beaten

pea purée (see page 208)

watercress

Venison kawakawa pie with smoked eel hash and minted pea purée. Marinate the venison for 24 hours for best results.

ACCOMPANIED WITH MONTEITH'S BLACK

PIE FILLING

Rub the kawakawa and crushed juniper into the venison and allow to marinate in the refrigerator for 24 hours. After marinating the venison, roll the meat in the seasoned flour, shaking off any excess. Heat half the oil in a frying pan and brown the meat with the garlic. Transfer to a heavy-bottomed saucepan or flame-proof casserole dish. Deglaze the pan with the red wine and pour over the meat. Add the stock. Bring to the boil and simmer gently till tender, about 2½ hours. If the sauce becomes too thick, add water to thin it down again. Remember the sauce needs to be thick enough when finished to hold as a pie. Remove from the heat and stir in the chocolate.

SMOKED EEL HASH

Cut the potatoes into roughly equal-sized pieces. Place in a pot, cover with water and season. Bring to the boil and cook until you can easily push a knife into the flesh. Drain the potatoes and allow to dry out. Do not let the potatoes go cold. In a separate pot, bring the cream to the boil and reduce by half. Melt in the butter. Mash the potatoes well with a potato masher, then pass through a sieve to remove any lumps. Add the butter and cream to the potatoes, and season with salt and white pepper. Remove the skin from the smoked eel or fish and finely chop the flesh. Using a fork, incorporate the eel into the mash.

PASTRY CASE

Grease a tin mould approximately 10 cm wide with the butter or oil. Loosely wrap the pastry around the outside of the mould to form a ring for the outer pie shape. Use the egg to secure the

Continued . . .

ends of the pastry, leaving a 3 cm overlap. Repeat till you have four pie rings. Bake at 200°C for 15 minutes, or until the pastry is golden brown and cooked all the way through.

ASSEMBLY

Place the pie case in the centre of the plate and three-quarters fill with the venison filling. Using a fork, gently cover the top of the pie with the hash, all the way out to the sides, being careful not to break the pie ring. Place a spoonful of pea purée on top of the pie, and garnish with watercress.

Note: You can use ready-made beef jus from your super-market to give a nice contrast in sauces and to make a stronger visual impact.

NOT SO BOARING BILLY GOAT BURGER

800 g goat mince
2 tbsp dried oregano
2 tbsp dried basil
3 tbsp wholegrain mustard
salt and pepper
4 rashers wild boar bacon
oil
4 Turkish pide
red onion relish (see page 216)
barbecue sauce (see page 214)
2 tomatoes
200 g Kapiti aged Cheddar
rocket leaves
fries (see page 212)

Seasoned goat patty with red onion relish and house-smoked barbecue sauce on grilled Turkish pide, served with fries.

ACCOMPANIED WITH MONTEITH'S CELTIC RED

Combine the mince, herbs, mustard and seasonings and mix well. Weigh out 200 g portions of the mix and shape into patties (not too fat for easier cooking). Sear the patties and bacon in a hot pan in a little oil or on a barbecue.

ASSEMBLY

Once your patties are cooked and you are ready to serve lightly grill the pide. Place a serving of the relish on one half and top with a patty, a slice of bacon and the barbecue sauce. Add some sliced tomatoes, Kapiti Cheddar and rocket and cover with another slice of the pide. Serve with a generous portion of fries and extra barbecue sauce on the side.

A DEERING ROULADE

VENISON ROULADE
800 g–1 kg venison
150 g salted butter
small bunch fresh mixed herbs, finely chopped
black pepper
3 cloves garlic, chopped
4 rashers streaky bacon
oil

MUSHROOM TARTE TATIN
2 shallots, diced
2 cloves fresh garlic, crushed
oil
4 field or portobello mushrooms, cubed
1 tbsp fresh parsley, chopped
½ tbsp fresh thyme, chopped
salt and pepper
1 sheet flaky pastry
1 egg whisked with water

red wine reduction (see page 224)
watercress or rocket leaves

Venison roulade filled with garlic and herb butter, wrapped in bacon, on a fried mushroom tarte Tatin with a rich red wine jus.

ACCOMPANIED WITH MONTEITH'S ORIGINAL

VENISON ROULADE

Preheat the oven to 200°C. Cut the venison into four even-sized pieces. Butterfly each piece of venison and lay on a clean bench or chopping board. With a meat tenderizer, tenderize the meat until it is an even 1 cm thickness all over. Mix the butter (at room temperature), herbs, pepper and garlic. Spread a layer of the butter over the venison. Roll the venison into a roulade with the butter mixture on the inside. Wrap with a rasher of bacon and tie a piece of butcher's string around to secure the bacon. Heat a frying pan with a little oil, brown all sides of the venison and place in the oven for 5–10 minutes, depending on how you like it cooked (5 minutes for rare, 10 minutes for well done). When cooked, remove from oven, cover with tinfoil and rest for 5 minutes.

MUSHROOM TARTE TATIN

In a frying pan, sauté the shallots and garlic in a little oil. Add the mushrooms, herbs, and salt and pepper. Continue to cook until the mushrooms have reduced in size and are soft. Place the mushroom mix into four individual flan dishes. Cut rounds of pastry the same size as the top of the flan dishes and place these on top of the mushroom mix. Glaze with the egg mix. Place in the oven for 15 minutes or until the pastry is golden and flaky.

ASSEMBLY

This attractive dish looks great on a long plate. Place the tarte Tatin on the plate. Cut off the untidy ends of the roulade and slice into 2 cm rounds. Place onto the plate and pour over the red wine reduction. Garnish with watercress or rocket.

OSCAR WILDE'S VENISON

BEER AND CHOCOLATE SOIL
oil spray
100 g butter
125 ml Monteith's Black
35 g dark cocoa powder
½ tsp salt
140 g flour
100 g sugar
½ tsp baking soda
1 egg
65 g sour cream

VENISON JUS
500 g venison bones
1 shallot
1 clove garlic
1 cup red wine
2 litres brown meat stock
small bunch fresh thyme
small bunch fresh rosemary
1 bay leaf
2 tbsp liquorice root
salt and pepper

BLACK KUMARA GNOCCHI
250 g black kumara
30 g potato
1 tbsp rock salt
2 tsp flour
1 tsp cornflour
1 tsp egg yolk
¼ tsp fine salt
pepper

A gentleman's dish of wild Fiordland venison, liquorice-infused jus, black kumara gnocchi, and Monteith's Black Beer and chocolate soil.

ACCOMPANIED WITH MONTEITH'S BLACK

MONTEITH'S BLACK BEER AND CHOCOLATE SOIL
Preheat the oven to 175°C. Line a loaf tin with baking paper and spray with oil. In a saucepan heat the butter, beer and cocoa powder until the butter melts, mix well and cool. Sift the dry ingredients together, add the beer-cocoa mixture and beat thoroughly with a whisk for 1 minute, then add the egg and sour cream. Continue to whisk for 2 minutes. Pour into a loaf tin and bake for 40 minutes. Place on a rack to cool completely and leave overnight. The next day, dice and blend the loaf in a food processor until the 'soil' (fine breadcrumbs) is formed.

LIQUORICE-INFUSED VENISON JUS
Make a traditional meat jus by roasting the venison bones in a pan, draining off the excess fat and adding sliced shallot and garlic. Add the red wine and reduce till syrupy. Cover with the brown meat stock, add the thyme, rosemary and bay leaf, and simmer gently for 4 hours. Strain through a fine sieve, then reduce down by two-thirds. Dry-roast the liquorice root in a 185°C oven for 10 minutes, crush with a mortar and pestle, then add it to the jus to infuse for 30 minutes. Strain through a fine sieve, taste and adjust the seasoning if necessary.

BLACK KUMARA GNOCCHI
Roast the kumara and potato on rock salt till cooked, then press through a sieve. Add the flours, yolk and salt, and mix to form a smooth dough. Roll into a tube, cut off 3½ cm lengths and reshape to form even tubes. Boil in salted water — when the gnocchi rise to the top of the water remove them and place on an oiled tray. Season.

Continued . . .

VEGETABLES

12 baby orange carrots
1 tbsp olive oil
¼ tsp sea salt
100 g cavolo nero, washed and
    sliced
clarified butter

4 x 120 g pieces wild venison
    loin, trimmed and rolled
    in plastic wrap into tubes,
    chilled
sea salt
clarified butter
100 g quince paste
fresh chervil

VEGETABLES

Peel and wash the carrots and pan fry with olive oil and sea salt. Be careful not to get any colour on the carrots. Pour over 1 cup boiling water, then cover with a lid and simmer gently for 10 minutes. Drain. In a very hot pan quickly sauté the cavolo nero with a little clarified butter and sea salt. Tip out onto paper towels and serve immediately.

VENISON

Unwrap the venison, season with sea salt, then roast in a hot pan with clarified butter. Cook till rare, then rest for 5 minutes and roll in Monteith's Black beer and chocolate soil.

ASSEMBLY

Slice each piece of venison into three, season with sea salt and place in the middle of the plate. Arrange the gnocchi, cavolo nero and carrots around the venison. Gently heat the quince paste in the microwave and place three dots onto each plate. Garnish with a piece of fresh chervil. Drizzle with jus and serve.

BUGS BUNNY COMES TO MATAMATA

1 cup feijoa flesh, stewed (or fresh kiwifruit)
2 bunches watercress
1 tsp sugar
2 orange kumara
3 tbsp olive oil
1 large red capsicum
2 tbsp manuka honey
1 tsp ground kawakawa
16 wild rabbit loins, silver skin removed (or pork)
salt
200 g goat feta

Pan-roasted wild rabbit with kumara and feta.

ACCOMPANIED WITH MONTEITH'S CRUSHED PEAR CIDER

Combine the stewed feijoa or fresh kiwifruit and watercress and blend until smooth. Taste, and if it's too sour add sugar. Dice the kumara into 1 cm cubes, add 1 tbsp olive oil and roast at 180°C until soft. De-seed the capsicum, and slice thinly. Place in a pan with 1 tbsp olive oil and cook on a medium heat until soft. Add the honey, cooked kumara and kawakawa. Turn the heat to low.

Heat a large pan with 1 tbsp oil until smoking hot, add eight rabbit loins and cook until slightly brown on one side, then turn over and brown again, around 1–2 minutes. Sprinkle with salt and set aside. Repeat this process with the second eight loins.

ASSEMBLY
Divide the kumara mixture between four heated plates. Stack the rabbit loins on the kumara. Crumble the feta over the top, add a spoonful of the feijoa or kiwifruit purée and garnish with watercress.

VENISON RACK

VENISON RACK

50 ml sesame seed oil

50 ml soy sauce

50 g honey

50 g brown sugar

zest and juice of 1 lemon

1 tbsp grated ginger

salt and pepper

1 x 1 kg venison French rack,
    cut to 4 portions

25 g lavender leaves

15 almonds

butter

JERUSALEM ARTICHOKE

12 Jerusalem artichokes

100 ml maple syrup

100 ml white wine

50 ml honey

pinch of turmeric

1 bay leaf

salt

TARO AND APPLE

4 apples

200 g taro

1 red onion

1 carrot

½ green banana

1 tsp sesame oil

zest of 1 lemon

¼ tsp ginger, chopped

salt and pepper

1 sprig thyme

150 ml cream

Lavender-crusted venison rack with a taro and green banana-filled apple, and goat cheese and kumara soufflé.

ACCOMPANIED WITH MONTEITH'S CELTIC RED

VENISON RACK

Blend the sesame seed oil, soy sauce, honey, brown sugar, lemon zest and juice, ginger, and a pinch of salt and pepper till smooth. Coat each portion of the venison rack with the marinade and set aside in a cool place for at least 30 minutes. Blend the lavender and almonds to a fine powder. Coat the marinated venison racks in the powder and fry in butter until golden. Place the racks in a 200°C oven and roast for 12–15 minutes.

JERUSALEM ARTICHOKE

Peel the artichokes and place in a shallow pan with the other ingredients and slowly sauté until soft.

TARO AND BANANA-FILLED APPLE

Cut the top off the apples and hollow them out. Dice the vegetables and banana and sauté them in the sesame oil. Season with the lemon zest, ginger, salt, pepper and chopped thyme. Add the cream to the vegetables, taking care to keep the mix comparatively thick. Fill the apples with the stuffing and bake in a moderate 160°C oven for 25 minutes.

Continued . . .

SOUFFLÉ

300 g golden kumara
1 clove garlic
pinch of turmeric
80 g goat cheese
150 ml cream
75 g flour
3 eggs, separated
salt
butter

red wine jus (see page 221)
redcurrant coulis (see page
  225)
lavender flowers
fresh mint leaves

GOAT CHEESE AND KUMARA SOUFFLÉ

Cook the kumara in salted water with the garlic and turmeric for 30 minutes. Drain and put through a sieve. Fold through the goat cheese, cream, flour, egg yolks, and salt, to taste. Whisk the egg whites to soft peaks and incorporate into the mixture. Grease moulds with butter and bake in a water bath at 130°C for 30 minutes.

ASSEMBLY

This dish with its many components looks great on a long plate or board. Arrange the items separately and drizzle a little red wine jus over the meat. Garnish with a few drops of redcurrant coulis, lavender flowers and mint leaves.

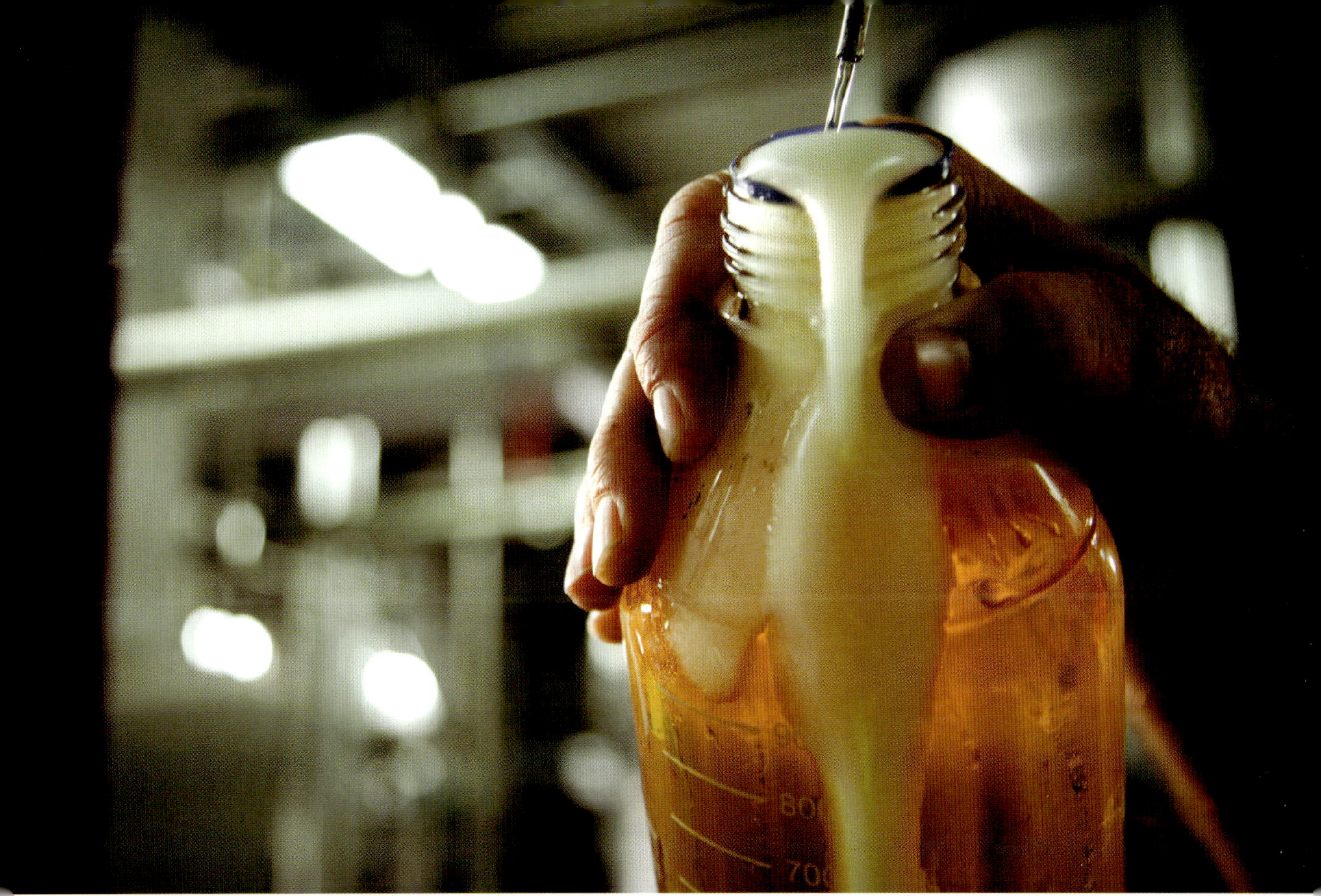
800

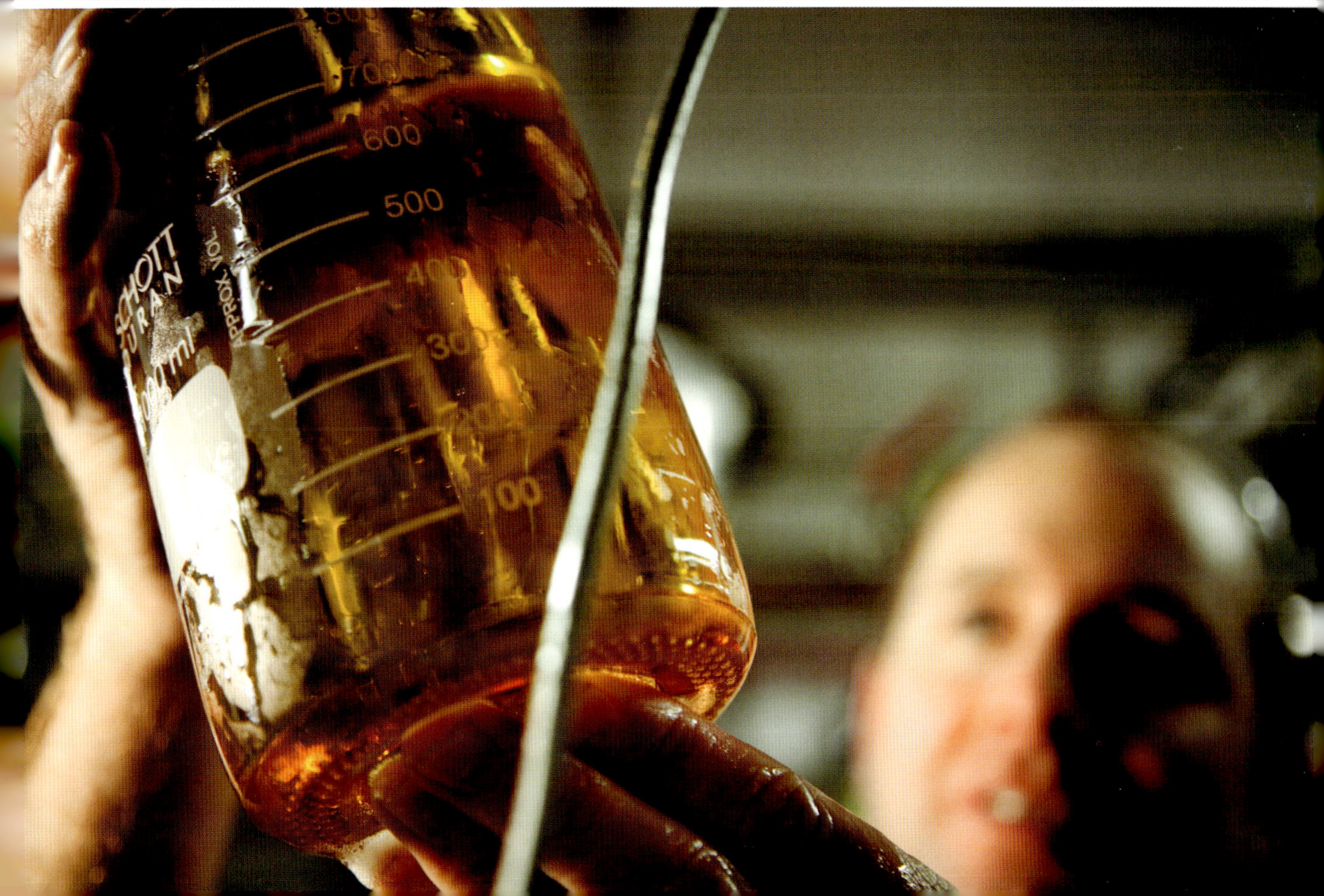
600
500
100
APPROX. VOL.

Beer and food matching

▸ **WILD PETER RABBIT**
with
MONTEITH'S PILSNER

———

▸ **TASTE OF SOUTHERN SEAS**
with
MONTEITH'S RADLER

———

◂ **FOUR WILD PIGS IN THE
ORCHARD**
with
**MONTEITH'S CRUSHED
APPLE CIDER**

———

▸ **WILD BOAR RAGOUT**
with
**MONTEITH'S SINGLE SOURCE
LAGER**

———

◂ **SMOKED FISH PIE**
with
**MONTEITH'S SINGLE SOURCE
LAGER**

———

▸ **XTREME GAME**
with
MONTEITH'S CELTIC RED

◄

PIE, DEER?

with

MONTEITH'S BLACK

►

**NOT SO BOARING BILLY GOAT
BURGER**

with

MONTEITH'S CELTIC RED

◄

A DEERING ROULADE

with

MONTEITH'S ORIGINAL

►

OSCAR WILDE'S VENISON

with

MONTEITH'S BLACK

◄

**BUGS BUNNY COMES TO
MATAMATA**

with

**MONTEITH'S CRUSHED
PEAR CIDER**

►

VENISON RACK

with

MONTEITH'S CELTIC RED

SMOKY RED DEER

1 tbsp olive oil

3 beetroot

salt

1 large potato

250 ml chicken stock

2 sprigs thyme

50 g butter

balsamic vinegar

manuka wood chips, for
   smoking

4 x 180 g venison loin

1 tbsp honey

1 tbsp black pepper, crushed

3 blood plums, chopped

20 g pistachio nuts, chopped

80 g baby spinach

red wine jus (see page 221)

1 tsp micro celery

1 stick fresh horseradish,
   peeled

Peppered wild red deer, smoked beetroot, plum and horseradish.

ACCOMPANIED WITH MONTEITH'S SINGLE SOURCE LAGER

Drizzle the olive oil over the beetroot and season with salt before wrapping each one in foil. Place the beetroot packages on a baking tray and roast in the oven at 190°C for 1–1½ hours or until tender. Unwrap the beetroot and rub the skins off with a cloth. Dice two of the beetroot into 1 cm cubes and reserve for smoking. Chop the remaining beetroot and reserve for the purée.

For the beetroot purée, dice the potato and cook in the chicken stock with the butter and half the thyme until tender (the chicken stock should reduce by two-thirds). Add the reserved beetroot and cook for 2 minutes. Purée in a blender until smooth. Season with salt and a dash of balsamic vinegar.

Cold-smoke the cubed beetroot with the manuka wood chips in a smoker for 20 minutes. Remove from the smoker, drizzle with olive oil, add the remaining thyme and reserve for later.

Season the venison with salt and seal all sides in a hot, oiled ovenproof pan until coloured. Roast in a 200°C oven for 3–4 minutes. Remove from the oven and add the honey to the pan, rolling the venison until well coated. Sprinkle liberally with the crushed black pepper, and rest for 2–3 minutes. While the venison is resting, gently stir-fry the smoked beetroot cubes in a little oil. After a minute add the chopped plums and pistachio nuts. Continue cooking for one more minute, then add the baby spinach and season with salt.

ASSEMBLY

Swipe the beetroot and potato purée across the plate by allowing the purée to fall off a spoon and then dragging the spoon through the purée. Arrange the smoked beetroot stir-fry alongside the purée. Slice the venison and lay beside the stir-fry. Spoon over the red wine jus, drizzle with a little olive oil, and finish with finely diced celery and freshly grated horseradish.

THE BLACK DUCK HOPPER

DUCK PROSCIUTTO
1–2 duck breasts
1 kg rock salt
4 pears, peeled
1 litre Monteith's Crushed
  Apple Cider
2 cinnamon quills
2 tbsp brown sugar

RABBIT RAGOUT ON RISOTTO
2 whole rabbits
2½ litres red wine
200 g celery, chopped
2 onions, chopped
2 carrots, chopped
6 cloves garlic, chopped
1 sprig rosemary
1 sprig thyme
1 bunch red grapes
salt and pepper
1 pack filo pastry
50–60 g shiitake mushrooms
150 g Arborio rice
1 litre vegetable stock
30 g Parmesan
30 g butter

BEER AND CHOCOLATE CAKE
3 litres Monteith's Black
200 g butter
8 eggs
700 g sugar
2 cups flour
30 g baking powder
300 g cocoa powder

250 g goat cheese

A tasting plate of duck prosciutto with goat cheese and Monteith's Crushed Apple Cider and pear purée; rabbit ragout with shiitake mushroom risotto; and Monteith's Black Beer cake. Note that curing and hanging your duck will take two weeks.

ACCOMPANIED WITH MONTEITH'S BLACK

DUCK PROSCIUTTO WITH PEAR AND CIDER PURÉE
Cure the duck in rock salt for three days, then wash off the excess salt. Hang it for two weeks until ready to serve. Poach the pears in Monteith's Apple Cider, cinnamon quills and sugar until soft. Purée until smooth.

RABBIT RAGOUT ON RISOTTO
Cut the rabbit in quarters and sauté in a hot pan, sealing every surface. Place the rabbit in a roasting pan, add the red wine, vegetables and herbs, cover with foil and braise at 180°C for 2 hours. Once cooled, remove all the meat from the bones and mix with the red grapes and seasoning and package up in filo baskets. Bake for 6–8 minutes. Top the parcel with a creamy shiitake mushroom risotto using Arborio rice, vegetable stock, Parmesan cheese and butter.

MONTEITH'S BLACK BEER AND CHOCOLATE CAKE
Reduce the beer by half with the butter. Whisk the eggs with the sugar till thick. Add the cooled reduction of beer. Add all the dry ingredients to the mix, pour into a lined tin, and bake for 45–60 minutes at 180°C.

ASSEMBLY
Use a large plate or board to show off all three components to their best. Place the thinly sliced duck prosciutto at one end. Sauce with apple cider purée and garnish with a crumble of goat cheese. Place the filo parcel of ragout and risotto, and lastly add a portion of the warm beer and chocolate cake to the plate. For a strong visual statement, try garnishing the cake with chopped red capsicum.

WHITE HEAT

1 medium–large white onion,
  roughly chopped
1 tbsp minced garlic
60 ml vegetable oil
3 heaped tbsp ground cumin
1–3 tbsp chilli powder, to taste
500 g turkey breast meat,
  minced
2 tbsp flour
salt and white pepper
1½ litres chicken stock
3 x 390 g can cannellini beans
3–4 fresh green chillies, finely
  chopped, to taste
green Tabasco sauce
spring onions
coriander
Cheddar cheese
corn chips

*A southern American variation on traditional chilli con carne,
replacing the usual red beef and kidney beans with turkey and
cannellini beans.*

ACCOMPANIED WITH MONTEITH'S SINGLE SOURCE LAGER

Sauté the onion and garlic in oil, taking care not to brown. Add
cumin and chilli powder and cook for a few minutes on a low
heat — do not let it burn. Add the turkey meat and sauté for a
few more minutes. Add flour, salt and pepper to taste and stir to
coat the meat. Add the stock, beans, chillies and Tabasco sauce.
Stir to combine and cook partly covered over a low to medium
heat for 1 hour, stirring occasionally. Adjust the seasonings to
suit.

ASSEMBLY
Serve with chopped spring onions, coriander and Cheddar
cheese, and a bowl of corn chips.

Note: This spicy recipe can easily be adjusted to suit. For
example, I add more cumin but it does make it go browner and
it loses some of that unique whiteness. You can also adjust the
number of green chillies. We like spicy food and so tend to
add a bit more, but you may choose to add less. The lower and
slower the cooking temperature and longer the cooking time,
the 'whiter' the chilli will be. You can always cook this dish the
day before and adjust the seasoning prior to serving, once the
flavours have settled.

BRUNCH THYME MUSHROOMS

6 large portobello mushrooms
20 g unsalted butter
50 g chorizo, very finely diced
1 red onion, very finely diced
1 large tomato, de-seeded and
  very finely diced
large bunch thyme
1 bottle Monteith's Black

Portobello mushrooms stuffed with chorizo and fresh thyme, poached in Monteith's Black — perfect for Sunday brunch with friends. The perfect beer match for this dish is Monteith's Black Rain: fill a glass half-full with Monteith's Black and top with champagne or any other good-quality sparkling wine.

ACCOMPANIED WITH MONTEITH'S BLACK

Preheat the oven to 180°C. De-stem the mushrooms and dice the stems finely. Set aside. Heat the butter and sauté the chorizo, onion and mushroom stems until soft. Fold in the tomato and a good handful of fresh thyme leaves. If the mix is too dry, add a splash of Monteith's Black. Heat through, taking care not to overcook. Place a generous spoonful of the mix into the cavity of each mushroom. Place the mushrooms into an ovenproof pan and drizzle over half the beer. Put in the oven and roast for about 10–15 minutes or until the mushrooms are just tender, checking frequently and basting with extra beer, if necessary.

ASSEMBLY

Garnish with a generous sprinkle of fresh thyme. Serve immediately.

BAMBI ON THE ROCKS

4 x 180 g venison loins

100 g fresh rock oysters

salt and pepper

150 g streaky bacon (manuka honey smoked)

5 large golden kumara, peeled

60 g butter

1 tsp ground horopito

20 baby carrots

6 leaves large savoy cabbage

1 tbsp honey

2 tsp parsley, chopped

2 litres beef stock

500 ml port

pesto (see page 214)

Wild venison carpet-bag loin and fresh New Zealand rock oysters wrapped in manuka honey smoked bacon, with sweet kumara and horopito purée, savoy cabbage, honey-glazed carrots, wild garlic pesto, and port wine jus.

ACCOMPANIED WITH MONTEITH'S SINGLE SOURCE LAGER

Begin by preparing the venison. Remove all sinew, but remember it is fine to leave some fat for flavour. Make slits in the side of the loins with a sharp knife and gently make a pocket big enough to slide your oysters into, but without cutting all the way through. Shuck the oysters and place them on paper towels to drain slightly. Season well with salt and pepper and stuff them into the venison loins. Wrap the venison loins with the streaky bacon, making sure to cover the slits.

Place the chopped kumara in a saucepan with plenty of salt and water, and bring to the boil for 10 minutes or until the kumara is very soft. Drain. Add half the butter, horopito, and salt and pepper. Place in a food processor and cream until smooth and velvety.

Sear the venison in a very hot ovenproof pan, ensuring that you crisp the bacon and also both sides of the loin. Place in a 200°C oven for 10 minutes.

Peel and blanch the carrots in rapidly boiling water for 5 minutes, drain and place in icy cold water to stop the cooking process. Do the same for the sliced savoy cabbage. Heat a little butter in a pan and add cold carrots, honey and seasoning and slowly cook until the carrots are warm and coated. Add a small knob of butter and chopped parsley. Toss in the cooked cabbage to warm it through.

For the jus, reduce the beef stock by half, add the port and reduce a further half. Add a small knob of butter.

ASSEMBLY

Position the venison in a large white dinner bowl. Place portions of the vegetables separately around the meat and add the jus. Garnish with the pesto.

BABBLING BROOK TO ROAR

PIKOPIKO SALSA
150 g red capsicum
olive oil
1 tsp rock salt
50 g pikopiko fronds
20 g red onion
100 ml avocado oil
1 tsp ground horopito

SMASH
300 g heritage potatoes
300 g red kumara
rock salt and pepper
olive oil
1 sprig wild thyme

SALAD
200 g smoked eel
zest and juice of ½ lemon
1 tsp parsley
50 g watercress
20 g butter

HOROPITO-ROASTED VENISON
600 g venison Denver leg
  (150 g per portion)
20 g ground horopito
20 g canola oil

caramel jus (see page 224)

Warm smoked eel on a watercress salad with char-grilled horopito-roasted venison, heritage potato and kumara smash and pikopiko and roast capsicum salsa, finished with a caramel jus.

ACCOMPANIED WITH MONTEITH'S BLACK

PIKOPIKO SALSA
Preheat the oven to 180°C. Roast the red capsicum with olive oil and a pinch of rock salt for 15–20 minutes until soft in texture. Remove from the oven, place in a bowl, cover and allow to cool in the fridge. Once the capsicum are cool enough to handle, peel away the skin and finely dice. Dice the pikopiko and red onion and combine with the capsicum in a bowl. Mix together the avocado oil, horopito and remaining rock salt and fold through the capsicum mix. Set aside.

ROAST POTATO AND KUMARA SMASH
Peel the potatoes and kumara, then dice them into small cubes. Place in a pot, cover with cold water, add salt and pepper and bring to a boil. Simmer until the potatoes and kumara are half-cooked. They should be firm but not raw. Preheat the oven to 180°C. Strain the potato and kumara and toss with olive oil, chopped wild thyme and seasoning. Place in a roasting tray and cook for 10–15 minutes until golden.

SMOKED EEL AND WATERCRESS SALAD
Make sure you take all the bones out of the eel, then flake it into a bowl. Add the lemon zest and juice, and freshly chopped parsley. Wash the watercress and set aside. On a low heat melt the butter in a pan and lightly sauté the smoked eel mix just to warm through. In a bowl, fold through the smoked eel with the watercress ready to serve.

Continued . . .

HOROPITO-ROASTED VENISON

This particular cut of meat is best eaten rare to medium rare. Preheat the oven to 200°C. Evenly coat the venison with the horopito and place in a preheated ovenproof pan with the oil. Cook for 5 minutes on each side or until evenly coloured. Remove from the heat and place in the oven. Bake for a further 7 minutes. Remove from the pan and rest for 4 minutes on a tea towel to catch any juices. Carve.

ASSEMBLY

Place three slices of the venison on a preheated plate. Add a generous spoonful of the smash and finish with the salsa. Add a serving of the eel and watercress. Spoon the heated jus over the venison and serve.

Beer and food matching

▶ SMOKY RED DEER
with
**MONTEITH'S SINGLE SOURCE
LAGER**

► THE BLACK DUCK HOPPER
with
MONTEITH'S BLACK

◀ WHITE HEAT
with
**MONTEITH'S SINGLE SOURCE
LAGER**

► BRUNCH THYME MUSHROOMS
with
MONTEITH'S BLACK

◀ BAMBI ON THE ROCKS
with
**MONTEITH'S SINGLE SOURCE
LAGER**

► BABBLING BROOK TO ROAR
with
MONTEITH'S BLACK

ORIGINAL ALE
(4.0% ABV)

Brewed to the same Monteith family recipe since 1868, Monteith's Original Ale is considered a pale ale in the heritage of beers brewed last century. By today's standards, Monteith's Original Ale is fairly dark and this illustrates how much beers have changed over time. In the 1700s, the average beer was very dark but since then beers have gradually become lighter in colour. On close inspection Monteith's Original Ale has a subtle blackberry aroma which originates from the female flowers of the Pacific Gem hops. Monteith's brewers have also been able to develop traditional yeasty fermentation characters and some fruity notes to the aroma. In terms of taste, it delivers a solid malty characteristic tending to the dark crystal malt range, with notes of caramel or burnt sugar. However, its key focus is extra bitterness, as the tradition of pale ales tends to be beers with significant hop characteristics. It's the hops that dominate aroma and taste. The blend of these characteristics creates a balance that reflects the historic style of pale ales — good body, complex ale fruitiness and a significant hoppy aftertaste.

Golden Lager
(5.0% ABV)

Monteith's Golden Lager is considered a malty lager in the heritage of beers traditionally brewed in parts of Germany. The Golden Lager is a rich golden colour, slightly darker than many other modern mainstream lagers. It has a refreshing fruity aroma, which contains a fresh natural yeastiness. The texture is smooth, and the taste sweeter, with just enough hops for a crispness to make it a really refreshing beer.

PILSNĚR beer.

(5.0% ABV)

Monteith's Pilsner is a Bohemian-style lager in the heritage of extremely hopped blonde beers brewed in parts of Eastern Europe. It has a complex hop aroma and a rich hop bitterness characteristic of this tradition in brewing, and challenges the perception of lagers being merely light and mild. The Pilsner taste has a malty quality that includes smooth caramel characteristics from the use of Vienna-style crystal malts, but the key notes derive from its enormous hop character. This tradition of highly hopped beers in New Zealand descends from the earliest days on the West Coast when hops were grown locally from Hokitika to Reefton and up to Motueka. Using a very special antique hop variety known as a 'noble hop', Monteith's brewers have been able to carefully balance intense hop aromas with smooth clean bitterness, which results in a natural freshness enhanced by the brewery's tradition of not pasteurizing to better preserve the natural traditional flavours.

CELTIC RED BEER

(4.4% ABV)

Monteith's Celtic Red is considered an Irish-style ale in the heritage of beers of a burnt-red colour traditionally brewed in the Emerald Isle. Monteith's brewers have been able to develop traditional ale fermentation characters while special kilning allows the interesting roasted malt notes to come through in the aroma. In terms of taste, the Celtic Red has a dry roasted malt flavour derived from the use of roasted chocolate malt and characteristic of this style of brewing. The hop character is only moderate, which allows the chocolate malts to show through, and the overall effect of the Celtic Red is of an invigoratingly dry, thirst-quenching beer.

black beer

(5.2% ABV)

Monteith's Black is in a league of its own in the heritage of very dark West Coast beers brewed prior to restrictions imposed on beers in New Zealand during World War II. Its distinction is in the rich smooth body that continues to develop as the beer is enjoyed. Its higher alcohol content than other mainstream black beers and its crisp dark maltiness are a result of using five different malts. Only a single hop variety is used and this allows the dry-roasted notes of darker malts to be balanced by the sweeter nutty tastes of the tawny malts.

With biscuit, nutty, caramel, chocolate and coffee malt characteristics, it's a special taste in beers that is truly akin to the rich black beers historically produced on the West Coast of New Zealand.

Monteith's Single Source Lager is a bottom-fermented batch-brewed straw-coloured Pilsner derived from Charmay barley from a single barley farm in Rakaia, and Southern Cross hops from a single Motueka hop farm. The result is a crisp, refreshing lager that is a reflection of climate, land and craft. The taste begins with a soft bitterness building delicately with an aromatic balance of citrus and spice, ending with a sharp, dry finish. You will recognize Monteith's Single Source as it is packaged in a black bottle protecting it from UV rays which are the enemy of good beer. A bottle of beer left exposed to sunlight or light from fluorescent bulbs significantly damages the taste of beer by altering the flavours of the delicate hops. This can yield a taste that is often described as 'skunky', and an aroma not unlike the skunk itself.

MONTEITH'S
SINGLE | SOURCE
LAGER BEER

(5.0% ABV)

Radler bier

(5.0% ABV)

Monteith's Radler is a refreshing, fruity, lemon-and-lime flavoured lager inspired by a drink first served up in Bavaria in the 1920s by Franz Xaver Kugler, the owner of an Austrian Gasthaus. In search of an invigorating brew, he developed an easy drinking lager with a citrus twist flavoured with lemon and lime, which was the perfect treat for the many cyclists (*Radler* in German) and mountain hikers who visited his alpine guesthouse. Monteith's Radler is brewed with a small amount of natural lemon juice, giving it its refreshing zesty citrus finish. This combination provides balance and a degree of complexity to the flavour mix — clean, crisp, slightly drying yet totally refreshing. Radler is only lightly hopped to ensure the bitterness character does not dominate the flavour.

CRUSHED APPLE CIDER
(4.5% ABV)

Monteith's Crushed Apple Cider is crafted from 100 per cent sun-ripened Nelson fruit from the province's many thousands of apple trees, rather than from concentrate. The apples are crushed to retain their natural flavour, so the cider is lighter, with full apple flavour and freshness.

CRUSHED PEAR CIDER
(4.5% ABV)

Monteith's Crushed Pear Cider is made purely with 100 per cent sun-ripened Nelson pears (not from concentrate) which are first crushed to release their juice, then directly fermented. The end result is a lighter and truer cider best served straight from the fridge.

Summer Ale

(5.0% ABV)

Monteith's Summer Ale is a bright gold beer made from four different malts spiced with a single hop variety and a touch of rata honey — subtle, but enough to make a difference.

It has a pleasing texture, a refreshing herbal spice taste and a quenching finish, and when served cold in the summer it is a great little thirst-quencher. A limited release over the summer months, Summer Ale is a refreshingly spiced beer with a real flavourful zest.

doppelbock Winter Ale

(6.0% ABV)

Doppelbock is a robust brew and was first brewed in the early 1600s to provide nourishment during the traditional German fasting periods, hence its affectionate nickname of 'liquid bread'. True to this heritage, Monteith's Doppelbock Winter Ale, with its fiery red hue, is subtly hopped by local varieties of the classic German Hallertau hop, typical in Bock-styled beers. This delivers a moderate to high bitterness but is mellowed on the palate by the full flavour from the blend of traditional German Munich-malts, Pilsner malt and dark malt used in brewing it. Released for the winter, Doppelbock Winter Ale is characterized by its smooth rich start, rounded body and long finish. Its hearty flavours are accentuated by the beer's elevated alcohol content, making it ideal for those looking for a comforting and tasty winter warmer.

Helpful hints for beer and food matching

LAGERS AND LIGHTER ALES

(e.g. Monteith's Golden Lager and Monteith's Summer Ale)
Mild lagers and lighter ales are great with food with more subtle flavours (like shellfish or chicken). However, if you are looking for a contrast, try these beers with spicy food or a good curry.

PILSNERS AND STRONG HOPPED BEERS

(e.g. Monteith's Pilsner and Monteith's Original Ale)
Dishes with herb flavours, tomato or capsicum sauces and those that use smoked ingredients are superb with more bitter beers. The distinct hop aroma and flavours complement the herbal and grassy ingredients in the dishes. Some Pilsners also work well with spicy food.

MALTY BEERS

(e.g. Monteith's Celtic Red and Monteith's Winter Ale)
The malty flavour and well-balanced bitterness of robust ale styles are ideal for the meat connoisseur. Enjoy these with lamb, beef, veal or even roast pork. Ales also go well with more strongly flavoured foods. Increase the seasoning or choose more strongly flavoured ingredients, and the beer flavour must also be more intense.

DARK BEERS

(e.g. Monteith's Black)
Dark beers are balanced by red meats in rich sauces and gravies. To establish your own benchmark, try a glass with a thick juicy steak cooked to perfection on the grill, or roast beef served with lashings of rich dark gravy. To appreciate how well old favourites have stood the test of time, try the traditional pairing of a dark beer with raw oysters. Dark beers also go with some cured meat such as corned beef served warm. Some of them, especially those with an identifiable fruitiness or caramel/toffee taste, also match well with desserts. Choose a dessert without too much flour and tending towards coffee and chocolate flavours. Remember: while it is possible to either complement or contrast your beer and food flavours, the overall quest is for synergy.

DESSERTS

HOTTER THAN A TART

¾ cup water

1 cup sugar

1 tsp crushed chilli (or store-bought chilli paste)

750 g bittersweet chocolate (minimum 50% cocoa solids)

300 g butter

9 eggs

chocolate mousse (see page 226)

raspberry compote (see page 226)

mascarpone

Flourless chocolate chilli tart with chocolate mousse and berry compote.

ACCOMPANIED WITH MONTEITH'S BLACK

Preheat the oven to 145°C. Grease a 20 cm round cake or flan tin. In a small saucepan over a medium heat combine the water, sugar and chilli. Stir until the sugar is completely dissolved. Melt the chocolate and butter together in a double boiler or the microwave. Mix until smooth. Beat in the hot sugar water, and then slowly beat in the eggs one at a time. Pour the cake batter into the prepared cake tin. Place the cake in the centre of the oven, and bake for 45 minutes or until the centre of the cake is just set. Remove from the oven and chill until firm before removing from the tin.

ASSEMBLY

Cut a wedge of the chocolate tart and serve with chocolate mousse, raspberry compote and a scoop of mascarpone.

CHOCOLATE CALZONE

1 ball pizza dough (see page 204)

flour, for dusting

¼ cup sugar

¾ cup semisweet chocolate chips

½ tsp vanilla extract

pinch of cinnamon

2 tsp shredded coconut

1 cup ricotta cheese

chocolate syrup

pecans, chopped

icing sugar

This is definitely not for the low-cal crowd, but the chocolate-loving sweet-eaters will certainly dig in! You can use pre-made pizza dough (enough for 1 x 32 cm crust) or pastry dough, or make the pizza dough on page 204. You can even use your bread machine.

ACCOMPANIED WITH MONTEITH'S BLACK

Preheat the oven to 230°C. Place the dough on a lightly floured surface. Press down and form into a circle. Using a floured rolling pin, roll the dough into a 32 cm circle, about 2–3 cm thick. Sprinkle with a pinch of sugar and press it into the dough. Cut the circle in half.

Mix the remaining sugar, chocolate chips, vanilla, cinnamon, coconut and ricotta. Place half of the mixture on each dough piece. Fold the dough over the filling. Cut the edges of the dough so that they are even. Seal the edges well with the tines of a fork. Fold approximately ¼ cm of the edge back over itself. Seal again with the fork, to be sure it's sealed well (or you'll have a real mess). Place on a lightly greased baking tray and bake until golden brown, approximately 8–10 minutes.

ASSEMBLY

Place a calzone on a large flat plate and drizzle chocolate syrup in a zigzag pattern over the top. Top with chopped pecans and icing sugar. If you feel the calzones are too big for single serves, cut them in half using a hot sharp knife.

FROMAGE BLANC

DOUSED MUSCATELS
120 g muscatels
240 ml cold water
240 ml muscat wine

FROMAGE BLANC
200 g mascarpone
130 g crème fraîche
170 g vanilla sugar (see page 225)
330 g thickened cream
170 g plain sweetened yoghurt
8 x 15 cm square pieces of muslin cloth and some string

STRAWBERRY SALAD
1 large punnet strawberries
½ cup icing sugar
3 tbsp lemon juice
fresh mint

HAZELNUT WAFERS
15 g flour
90 g caster sugar
100 g ground hazelnuts
2 egg whites
20 ml hazelnut oil

Fromage blanc with muscatels, strawberry salad and a hazelnut wafer. I love this dessert; it has a perfect balance of texture and flavour. The smooth and creamy fromage is sweet with acidic undertones, the berries introduce the freshness of the season and the hazelnut wafer provides a wonderful nutty crunch. Note that you will need to start this recipe two days before you intend serving it.

ACCOMPANIED WITH MONTEITH'S CRUSHED PEAR CIDER

DOUSED MUSCATELS

First separate the muscatels from the stalks and soak them overnight in water. This will allow them to soften and swell. They are better stored in the fridge. On the day you make the fromage blanc, strain the water from the muscatels and discard it. Soak the muscatels in the muscat wine, and once again leave them in the fridge overnight until you are ready to use them. The longer you leave them, the better the flavour.

Note: You don't have to use muscat wine; your favourite sticky will be just fine, but true muscat is well worth the investment.

FROMAGE BLANC

Combine the mascarpone, crème fraîche and vanilla sugar in a large stainless-steel bowl and work it around the surface of the bowl with a rubber spatula until it is perfectly smooth. In a separate, smaller bowl combine the thickened cream and yoghurt, then add this to the larger bowl and combine until it is beautifully smooth. Divide the fromage into eight 125 g portions, placing each portion onto the centre of a square of muslin cloth. Pull the corners up around the fromage to form a ball and tie them off, leaving a long tail of string so that they can be tied to a rack in the fridge and hung overnight. Be sure to have a catching tray underneath as they will purge some liquid.

Note: The fromage blanc will keep for a couple of days but it is much better served the day after it is made.

Continued . . .

STRAWBERRY SALAD

This recipe is a very simple way to marinate strawberries that will also produce a delicious sauce for your dessert. I love to finish this salad off with a good amount of torn mint.

Trim and quarter the strawberries and fold in the icing sugar until shiny and glazed. Add lemon juice and leave to marinate for about 30 minutes, then fold through the mint. If you would like more sauce, add more icing sugar and lemon juice. A good guide to maintain the correct balance is approximately three parts sugar to one part lemon juice, e.g. 1 tbsp icing sugar to 1 tsp lemon juice.

HAZELNUT WAFERS

This recipe will make many more than eight wafers, so you can keep the batter in the fridge for up to two weeks and whip up a little treat to go with a bowl of ice cream whenever you feel like it.

Sift the flour into a medium-sized mixing bowl, then add the sugar and hazelnuts and mix it all together. Lightly whisk the egg whites until they just begin to foam, then fold them into the dry ingredients with a rubber spatula and finally add the oil. The batter needs to be rested at room temperature for 1 hour before it's cooked. Preheat your oven to 220°C.

To cook the wafers, spread a thin layer of the batter into whatever shapes you like onto a tray lined with baking paper. Bake them until they are golden brown; this should take 4–5 minutes. Give the wafers about a minute to firm up, then gently lift them off the paper and allow to cool.

ASSEMBLY

Carefully unwrap each ball of fromage blanc and place in the centre of eight shallow dessert bowls. Spoon some of the strawberries around the bowls, and divide the sauce evenly. Garnish with the muscatels. Stick a wafer into the side of each dessert and you're done.

SWEET PASSION

3 ripe bananas
190 g soft butter
190 g caster sugar
3 eggs
¼ tsp vanilla essence
115 g self-raising flour
¾ tsp baking powder

BUTTERSCOTCH SAUCE
300 ml cream
400 g brown sugar
200 g soft butter

passion fruit syrup (see page 225)
mascarpone
hokey pokey (see page 226)

Roast banana pudding with butterscotch sauce, passion fruit syrup and hokey pokey.

ACCOMPANIED WITH MONTEITH'S BLACK

Preheat the oven to 200°C. Lay the unpeeled bananas on a tray and cook until their skins turn black and the flesh is very soft. Remove the flesh and allow to cool. Cream the butter and sugar, and whisk in the eggs one at a time. Add the banana and the vanilla essence, then sift and fold in the dry ingredients to form a soft batter.

To make the butterscotch sauce, bring the cream to a simmer and add the sugar, stirring to dissolve. Add the butter and gently simmer to form a smooth, rich sauce. This sauce can be kept in the fridge for up to a week and simply reheated in the microwave.

Lightly grease ramekins with soft butter, then spoon a couple of tablespoons of butterscotch sauce into each one. Three-quarters fill the ramekins with the banana batter then place them in a deep roasting pan. Add enough hot water to the roasting pan to come halfway up the sides of the ramekins. Bake the banana puddings at 150°C until the tops are dark golden brown and a skewer comes out clean. Remove the puddings from the water and allow them to rest for 10 minutes before turning them out of the ramekins. Leave on a cooling rack until you need them.

Note: I prefer to serve mine warm, so I cook them during the day and give them a quick zap in the microwave when we are ready for dessert.

ASSEMBLY
Place the warm pudding onto a plate. Spoon two tablespoons of warm butterscotch sauce over the pudding. Drizzle a little passion fruit syrup around the plate. Serve with a scoop of mascarpone and a chunk of homemade hokey pokey.

Note: If passion fruit are in season, cut one in half and serve it on the side, or scoop the flesh out on top of the pudding.

SWEET MEATS

70 g sugar

330 ml double cream

3 egg yolks

165 g good-quality dark
  chocolate (e.g. Callebaut)

30 ml coffee

30 ml cognac

4 sheets filo pastry

melted butter

icing sugar

50 g redcurrants or
  blackcurrants

50 g sugar

1 tbsp water

4 x 80 g venison fillets, thinly
  sliced

good-quality olive oil

mint or edible flowers

Venison carpaccio with filo and crème au chocolate, served with a berry sauce.

ACCOMPANIED WITH MONTEITH'S BLACK

Combine the sugar and cream in a saucepan and simmer for 2–3 minutes. Beat the egg yolks in a bowl or electric mixer. While beating, pour the sugar and cream mixture in a slow stream along the side of the bowl. Melt the chocolate over a double boiler and pour into a clean bowl. Fold in the yolk and cream mixture, followed by the coffee and cognac, until just incorporated. Transfer into a piping bag and set aside in the refrigerator for 2 hours.

Preheat the oven to 175°C. Brush each sheet of filo pastry with butter and dust with icing sugar. Stack the sheets, then cut into 12 squares. Bake for 6–7 minutes until golden.

For the berry sauce, cook the currants, sugar and water in a small saucepan for 2–3 minutes. Set aside to cool.

ASSEMBLY

Place the venison in the centre of the plate. Brush the meat with oil and dust it with icing sugar. Place one square of filo on top of the meat, then pipe the chocolate crème on top of the filo. Add another square of filo and chocolate and then a third so that you have three layers. Garnish with the berry sauce and fresh mint or edible flowers. Serve.

CHEEKY TART

5 large feijoas

200 g sugar

juice of 2 lemons

4 Cox's Orange Pippin apples

60 ml Calvados

20 g butter

100 g puff pastry (store-
bought is fine)

100 g walnuts

100 ml cream

vanilla ice cream

apple mint

1 Granny Smith apple

Apple and feijoa tart with vanilla ice cream and Calvados caramel sauce.

ACCOMPANIED WITH MONTEITH'S CRUSHED APPLE CIDER

Peel and dice the feijoas into small cubes. Caramelize 30 g sugar in a pan, add the feijoas and cook for 2–3 minutes. Add a squeeze of lemon, set aside and allow to cool.

Peel the Cox's apples and cut into chunky slices. Caramelize 50 g sugar in a pan, add the apples and cook for 2 minutes, tossing all the time. Remove from the pan and set aside. Deglaze the pan with 20 ml Calvados, add the butter and cook until glazed. Add to the resting apples.

Roll out the puff pastry to a 6 mm thickness. Cut into rectangular shapes. Prick these with a fork and bake at 180°C between two trays for 12–14 minutes or until golden.

Caramelize 60 g sugar in a pan and add the walnuts, stirring until well coated. Tip onto a tray and allow to cool. When fully cooled, place in a blender and crush to a fine powder.

For the Calvados sauce, caramelize the remaining sugar in a pan and then deglaze with the rest of the Calvados and the juice of one lemon. Add the cream and reduce until thickened.

To build the tarts, spoon some of the feijoa on top of the puff pastry, then arrange the caramelized apple slices on top. Place in a 180°C oven for 4–6 minutes or until hot.

ASSEMBLY

Drizzle the sauce onto the dessert plate. Place the tart on top of the sauce. Place the praline next to the tart and place a scoop of ice cream on top. Arrange mint and freshly sliced Granny Smith apple over the dish and serve.

Beer and food matching

◄ **HOTTER THAN A TART**
with
MONTEITH'S BLACK

───────────

► **CHOCOLATE CALZONE**
with
MONTEITH'S BLACK

───────────

◄ **FROMAGE BLANC**
with
**MONTEITH'S CRUSHED
PEAR CIDER**

───────────

► **SWEET PASSION**
with
MONTEITH'S BLACK

───────────

◄ **SWEET MEATS**
with
MONTEITH'S BLACK

───────────

► **CHEEKY TART**
with
**MONTEITH'S CRUSHED
APPLE CIDER**

───────────

Two bowl bread

MAKES 2 MEDIUM-SIZED LOAVES

BOWL ONE

1 tbsp golden syrup
2 cups boiling water
1 cup milk
1 cup Monteith's Black
1 tbsp yeast granules (look for
  the yellow-top container)

BOWL TWO

500 g white flour
500 g wholemeal flour
2 tsp salt
3 tbsp bran flakes

BOWL ONE

Dissolve the golden syrup in the boiling water. Add the cold milk and beer. Sprinkle the yeast granules on top. Cover with a tea towel and set aside for 5 minutes.

BOWL TWO

Sift and stir together the flours, salt and bran flakes. Add the wet ingredients and stir well. Divide the mixture into two well-greased medium-sized loaf tins. Place into the middle of a cold oven. Use the lowest setting, no higher than 50°C, and cook for 30 minutes or until a skewer placed into the centre of the bread comes out clean. Increase the oven temperature to 180°C and bake for 30 minutes. Place on a rack until the bread cools, or you can enjoy it while it's still warm.

Brioche

MAKES 4

1 cup warm water
2 tbsp warm milk
1 tsp active dry yeast
1½ tbsp sugar
2 cups bread flour
1 tsp salt
1¼ tbsp unsalted softened
  butter
2 large eggs
2 tsp sesame seeds (optional)

Preheat the oven to 160°C (fan bake). In a glass measuring cup combine the water, milk, yeast and sugar and stand until foamy. In a large bowl mix the flour with the salt, then add the butter and rub to make crumbs. Stir in the yeast mixture and one beaten egg until a dough forms. Scrape the dough onto a well-floured bench and knead until smooth and elastic (8–10 minutes). The dough will be sticky, but keep in mind the more flour you knead in the tougher the buns will be. Shape the dough into a ball and return to the bowl. Cover with plastic wrap and leave in a warm place until it has doubled in size (1–2 hours). Divide the dough into four equal parts, gently roll each into a ball and place them on a tray about 5 cm apart. Cover and rise for another hour. Lightly beat the second egg, add 1 tsp cold water and use a pastry brush to lightly brush the buns with the egg wash. Sprinkle with sesame seeds and place on a tray in the middle of the oven. Cook for 20 minutes until golden brown.

Pizza dough

1 cup warm water (40°C)
7 g package dry yeast
3¼ cups flour
1 tsp salt
¼ cup olive oil, less 2 tbsp
   measured out separately

Note: If using a bread machine, instead of mixing the yeast and water, first place the water in the pan of the machine. Then add 2 tbsp olive oil, flour, salt and yeast, in that order.

Place the water in a small bowl. Add the yeast and stir — a beige mixture should form. Stand for approximately 5 minutes or until a light layer of foam forms on top. In a large mixing bowl combine 3 cups of the flour and the salt. Make a well in the centre, and add the yeast mixture and oil. Stir the dry ingredients into the liquid until it is well mixed and a soft dough forms. Turn the dough onto a floured work surface and knead, slowly adding the remaining ¼ cup flour, until the dough is no longer sticky. Knead just until the dough is smooth and elastic and all visible flour is incorporated. Shape the dough into a ball, and place into another bowl oiled with the 2 tbsp of remaining oil. Roll the ball around to coat evenly. Cover the bowl with plastic wrap, place in a warm, draught-free location, and allow to rise until doubled in size. Punch down and knead for another minute on a floured board before using.

Choux pastry

1 cup water
½ cup unsalted butter, cut into
   2 cm pieces
1 tsp salt
1 cup all-purpose flour
4 large eggs

Boil the water, butter and salt in a saucepan. Add the flour and work the mixture together over a low heat. Remove from the heat and add the eggs one at a time, beating well with a wooden spoon after each addition.

Fresh pasta

200 g pasta flour
100 g fine semolina (or
  high-gluten flour)
6 egg yolks
1 whole egg

Mix the flour and semolina on a clean surface and make a well in the centre. Add the egg yolks and egg and mix them with a fork, bringing the flour to the middle, until you have formed enough of a dough to mix it by hand. Knead it well until you have formed a smooth, elastic dough. This should take about 5 minutes of hard labour. If the dough is too sticky add more flour, or if it is too dry add a little of the egg whites. Wrap the dough in plastic wrap and rest it in the fridge for 30 minutes. Cut the dough into two pieces and work with only one at a time; keep the other half covered under a damp cloth.

Your unused pasta will stay fresh in the fridge for about half a day, then you can roll it into ribbons, e.g. pappardelle or tagliatelle. Dry it by hanging it over a coat hanger for a couple of days in a dry place until you can crumble it in your hand, then you can store it in an airtight container for up to two months.

Caramelized shallots

1 tsp olive oil
2½ cups diced shallots
20 g butter
Maldon sea salt
freshly ground black pepper

Heat a saucepan until hot. Add the olive oil, closely followed by the diced shallots. Reduce the heat and gently sweat the shallots (cook without browning). Once the shallots are softened, add the butter. Increase the heat to a medium setting, then allow the natural sugars from the shallots to slightly brown on the bottom of the pan (around 20 minutes). Remove the saucepan from the heat and leave for 2 minutes to deglaze the sediment. Stir all of the browned sediment together with the shallots. Return to the heat for further browning (around 10 minutes), remove from the heat for further deglazing, and repeat this cycle at least half a dozen times or until you are happy with the colour and flavouring. Season with salt and pepper.

Cider-braised onions

SERVES 4 AS A SIDE

2 large brown onions
1 tbsp oil
1 bottle Monteith's Crushed
   Apple Cider
2 tbsp brown sugar

Preheat the oven to 165°C. Remove the ends and skins of the onions and slice lengthways. In an ovenproof frying pan add the oil and bring to a medium heat. Add the onions and cook until soft. Add one bottle of Monteith's Crushed Apple Cider and the sugar, cover with tinfoil and place in the oven for 30–40 minutes or until the liquid has reduced and the onions are sticky.

Roasted shallots

SERVES 4 AS A SIDE

6 shallots, skin on
6 sprigs thyme
2 cloves garlic, skin on
pinch of flaky sea salt
pinch of cracked white pepper
2 tbsp olive oil

Toss all the ingredients together and wrap them into a bundle using tinfoil. Bake at 180°C for about 45 minutes or until the shallots are tender. Allow to cool, then peel and set aside. This can be done up to two days in advance if you store them in the fridge in an airtight container.

Roasted beetroot

SERVES 4 AS A SIDE

3 large beetroot
salt and pepper
2 tbsp canola oil

Half-fill a medium-sized pot with water and add 2 tbsp salt (this helps the beetroot keep its colour). Add the beetroot and boil for 20 minutes or until the beetroot softens. Remove from the heat and run under cold water. Remove the skins and stalks from the beetroot. Place the peeled beetroot on an oven dish, season with salt and pepper and add the canola oil. Place in a preheated 190°C oven for 15–20 minutes, then cool and refrigerate.

Garlic confit

3 whole heads garlic, skin on
16 shallots, skin on
500 ml olive oil

Place the garlic, shallots and oil in an ovenproof dish and cover with tinfoil. Bake in the oven at 50°C for 3 hours.

Pea purée

SERVES 4 AS A SIDE

200 g green peas
4 mint leaves
pinch of salt
pinch of sugar

Place the peas in a pot and add just enough water to cover them. Smash the mint leaves between the palms of your hands to release the oils, and add to the peas along with the salt and sugar. Bring to the boil and remove from the heat. Drain off the water into a separate container. Purée the peas in a blender, adding just enough cooking liquid to give a silky-smooth consistency. Strain through a sieve to remove any lumps.

Parsnip purée

SERVES 4 AS A SIDE

½ onion, chopped
2 cloves garlic, crushed
butter
500 g parsnips, peeled and
  chopped, cores removed
200 ml milk
100 ml cream
salt and white pepper

Sauté the onion and garlic in a saucepan with a little butter. Add the parsnip and milk and cover with water. Simmer for about 15 minutes or until tender. Strain off the liquid and then blend while hot in the food processor for about 5 minutes, adding cream and salt and white pepper to taste.

Butternut purée

SERVES 4 AS A SIDE

320 g butternut pumpkin
salt and pepper
1 tsp brown sugar
50 g butter

Peel and dice the pumpkin into large cubes. Season with salt, pepper and brown sugar. Steam or lightly sauté in butter. Place in a food processor and purée, then pass through a fine sieve.

Cauliflower and Persian purée

SERVES 4 AS A SIDE

½ cauliflower
1 onion, chopped
4 cloves garlic, chopped
2 tbsp butter
1 tsp Persian spice (or allspice)
150 g crème fraîche
1 tbsp manuka honey
zest of 1 lemon
juice of ½ lemon
salt and pepper

Cook the cauliflower in salted water until tender, and drain. Sauté the onions and garlic in a pan in butter until lightly coloured. Add the cauliflower and sauté until the cauliflower is lightly browned. Place in an ovenproof dish and sprinkle over the Persian spice. Roast at 180°C for 30 minutes, then place in a food processor with crème fraîche, honey, and lemon zest and juice. Blend until a smooth purée forms. Add salt and pepper to taste.

Kumara dauphinoise

SERVES 4 AS A SIDE

1 kg red kumara, peeled
1 tsp salt
½ tsp white pepper
500 ml cream
100 g grated cheese

Peel and thinly slice the kumara and place in a bowl. Add salt, white pepper and half of the cream and mix well. Evenly layer the sliced kumara into a small roasting dish, slowly building up layers to fill the dish. Once all the kumara is used, pour over the rest of the cream and top with grated cheese. Cover with tinfoil and bake at 200°C for 1¼ hours (for the last 15 minutes remove the tinfoil) or until a knife will easily insert into the centre of the dauphinoise. For a more professional look when serving, the dauphinoise can be pressed with a weight on top while setting in the fridge and simply reheated when required.

Potato dauphine

SERVES 4 AS A SIDE

500 g potatoes, peeled
choux pastry (see page 204)
100 g feta, crumbled
salt
¼ tsp grated nutmeg
oil, for frying

Cut the potatoes into large cubes and boil until tender. Drain and put through a ricer. Combine the potatoes, choux pastry and feta. Mix well. Season to taste with salt and nutmeg. Preheat oil for deep frying to 160°C. Spoon the potato mixture into a pastry bag fitted with a plain ½ inch tip. While pressing the mixture out, cut into round balls and carefully drop into the hot oil. Do not overload the fryer. After a few minutes, the potatoes will puff and float, and turn golden brown. Transfer to a tray lined with paper towels to absorb the oil, and keep warm.

Rustic vegetables

SERVES 4 AS A SIDE

1–2 parsnips
1–2 kumara
1–2 potatoes
6–8 purple potatoes
1 onion, diced
olive oil
salt and pepper

Peel the parsnip, kumara and potatoes and cut into chunky wedges. Place in a roasting dish with diced onion and drizzle with olive oil. Season with salt and pepper and roast at 180°C for 30–40 minutes.

Fries

SERVES 4 AS A SIDE

6 potatoes, peeled
oil, for frying

This is a sure-fire way of making great fries every time. Cut approximately 5 mm thick strips of potato and blanch in a deep fryer. Drain and store in the fridge. Just before serving, re-fry in hot oil until crispy, drain and season.

Wild pork mousse

250 g wild pork trimmings
200 ml cream
pinch of flaky sea salt
pinch of cracked white pepper

Blend the wild pork for about 10 seconds in a food processor, then add the cream and the seasonings while the blender is still running. Blend for a further 30 seconds until the mix is smooth. Use a spatula to remove the mousse from the blender bowl and pass it through a sieve with a pastry card.

Smoke mix

1 cup rice
1 cup brown sugar
1 cup loose fruit-infused tea
  leaves

Combine all ingredients and store. It will last up to two weeks if sealed in an airtight jar, but it's best used straight away.

Aioli

MAKES 350 G

8 sprigs thyme
1 head garlic, skin on
1 tsp flaky sea salt
350 ml canola oil
2 egg yolks
½ tsp white pepper
1 tbsp Dijon mustard
juice of ½ lemon

Place the thyme on a sheet of tinfoil with the garlic head. Add a pinch of sea salt and 1 tbsp canola oil and fold into a parcel. Place in a 160°C oven, checking every 10 minutes for 30–40 minutes (or until the garlic is soft). In a medium-sized bowl place the egg yolks, ½ tsp sea salt, white pepper, mustard and lemon juice. Using an electric beater or whisk combine until thick. While whisking slowly add the remaining oil; the mixture will thicken. Be careful not to add the oil quickly or it will split. Once the garlic is soft and chilled, remove the skins, chop finely and add to the mayonnaise base. Mix well, cover and refrigerate.

Pesto

MAKES 225 G

30 g wild garlic leaves
50 g basil leaves
2 cloves fresh garlic
2 tsp lemon juice
125 ml extra virgin olive oil
salt and pepper

Combine all the ingredients in a food processor and process until well mixed. Avoid making it too smooth, as it works better when a little chunky.

Barbecue sauce

MAKES 750 G

1 white onion
1 clove garlic
1 tbsp olive oil
300 ml dark soy sauce
100 g brown sugar
300 ml tomato sauce
25 g liquid smoke (optional)

Purée the onions and garlic in a food processor, then sweat them in oil till soft. Add the soy sauce and sugar, bring to a boil and simmer for 15 minutes. Remove from the heat, and add the tomato sauce then the liquid smoke, if you are using it.

Granny Smith apple sauce

MAKES 750 G

2 tbsp butter
1 sprig rosemary
70 g caster sugar
375 ml dry white wine
4 Granny Smith apples
2 cloves
2 black peppercorns
1 cinnamon quill

Heat a small saucepan to a medium–high heat and add the butter. When it begins to foam and change to a light-brown colour, add a sprig of rosemary and remove the pan from the heat. Pass the brown butter through a sieve and leave it at room temperature until it is ready to be added to the apple sauce.

Melt the sugar in the wine over a gentle heat. Peel and core the apples and cut into quarters. Stud one of the apple pieces with the cloves and peppercorns, then add all the apples and the cinnamon quill to the wine and cover with a round of baking paper. Cook over a high heat until the wine has evaporated and the apples are very tender and opaque (be careful not to let the apples caramelize at all). Remove the spices. Purée the apples in a blender with the brown butter until it is pale and smooth, and set it aside. This recipe can be made two days in advance if it is stored in an airtight container in the fridge.

Red onion relish

MAKES 400 G

2 red onions, sliced
1 clove garlic, crushed
100 g brown sugar
35 ml red wine vinegar
35 ml white wine vinegar
20 g sultanas
1 tsp tomato paste

Place all the ingredients in an appropriate-sized pot, cover with water and simmer until a smooth and shiny consistency is achieved.

Red onion and fennel salad

SERVES 4 AS A SIDE

1 red onion, finely sliced
½ fennel bulb, finely shaved
¼ red capsicum, finely sliced
¼ cup fried sage leaves
salt and pepper
olive oil

Mix all the ingredients together, season and drizzle with olive oil.

Spiced pear and ginger relish

MAKES 200 G

1 tbsp mustard seeds, soaked
½ cup raw sugar
125 ml cider vinegar
1 onion, chopped
2 pears, peeled and diced
100 g crystallized ginger, diced
1 tbsp ground horopito
2 cloves garlic, thinly sliced
½ tsp caraway seeds
1 cinnamon quill

Place all the ingredients in a saucepan and simmer gently for around 3 hours.

Tomato fondue

MAKES 1 LITRE

1 cup olive oil
1 bunch basil
8 shallots, finely sliced
4 cloves garlic, finely sliced
large pinch of flaky sea salt
¼ tsp freshly cracked white
   pepper
1 kg whole peeled tomatoes
pinch of sugar

Bring the oil to a moderate heat, then sizzle the basil in the oil until it becomes transparent. Remove and discard the basil. Gently cook the shallots and garlic in the basil-scented oil until they become tender, then add the salt and pepper and the tomatoes. Add about a cup of water to the sauce. Cook the sauce gently for about 1 hour, then season with a pinch of sugar and more salt if needed. Purée the sauce in a blender, then pass it through a fine sieve. This sauce can be made a few days in advance if you store it in the fridge in an airtight container. This recipe can also be used as a soup or a pasta sauce.

Fish stock

MAKES 2 LITRES

40 g unsalted butter
1 small onion, finely diced
1 small stick celery, finely diced
4 white peppercorns
1 small bay leaf (fresh or dry)
4 parsley stalks
juice of ½ lemon
1½ kg fish head and bones
   (one washed, medium-sized
   snapper carcass will do)
1½ cups white wine
8 cups cold water

Melt the butter in a deep saucepan and lightly fry the onion and celery until they appear opaque. Add the peppercorns, herbs and lemon juice and cook for 2 minutes. Add the chopped fish bones, cover with a tight lid and gently stew for 5 minutes. Add the wine and water, bring to a simmer, skim off the foam and continue to simmer for 20 minutes. Remove from the heat. Sit for 20 minutes and strain through a fine sieve.

Lemon-infused vegetable stock

1 litre vegetable stock
2 lemons, quartered

Bring the vegetable stock to the boil with the lemons and simmer on a low heat for 45 minutes. Top up with water as you go to make 1 litre of lemon stock. Keep the stock warm while you are using it.

Fish velouté

MAKES 500 ML

50 g unsalted butter
½ small onion, finely diced
½ tbsp sea salt
50 g flour, sifted
2 cups hot fish stock (see page 219)

Melt the butter in a deep saucepan and lightly fry the onions and salt until the onions appear opaque. Add the flour and mix well using a wooden spatula. Cook the roux on a low heat until it becomes a light-golden colour with a sandy texture, then remove it from the heat. Slowly add the hot fish stock, stirring continuously with a whisk to avoid lumps. Cook on a low heat for 30 minutes and stir occasionally to avoid sticking.

Red wine jus

MAKES 400 ML

1 litre beef stock
200 ml red wine
salt and white pepper

Reduce the beef stock and red wine to around 300–400 ml (a thin sauce consistency). Add salt and white pepper to taste.

Monteith's Celtic Red jus

MAKES 150–200 ML

1 small onion
1 stick celery
1 small carrot
1 tsp black peppercorns
1 tsp fennel seeds
oil
100 ml red wine
150 ml Monteith's Celtic Red
150 ml game or beef stock
50 ml beef glaze
salt and pepper

Roughly dice the vegetables. Brown the vegetables, peppercorns and fennel seeds in a little oil. Add the red wine and reduce until it is almost gone. Add the beer and reduce by half. Add the stock and beef glaze and reduce by about a third. Taste, and add salt and pepper if required.

Madeira jus

2½ kg chicken bones (ask your local butcher)

4 tbsp canola oil

4 ripe tomatoes, roughly chopped

1 bunch parsley

2 bay leaves

2 carrots, diced

2 small onions, sliced

½ leek (white with a little green), washed and chopped

1 stick celery, chopped

4 cloves garlic, skin on, crushed

2 cups Madeira port

2 sprigs thyme

cracked pepper

Note: This process can be done over two days, the extraction on day one and the reduction on day two. This jus will go a long way, but if you need more you can double the quantity of ingredients and increase the cooking time by about a third.

Preheat the oven to 250°C. Chop the chicken bones up into thumb-size pieces and place them on an oiled roasting tray. The tray should be large enough so that the bones don't overlap. Roast the bones for about 45 minutes, then turn them over and roast for a further 45 minutes until they are dark golden. Remove from the oven and place in a 10 litre capacity pot.

Deglaze the roasting tray by adding 2 cups of hot water and bringing it to a slow simmer, taking care to scrape up all of the crusty bits and stir them through the liquid. Add this liquid to the pot with the bones. Double the volume of liquid in the pot by adding water and bring it to a fast simmer. While it is simmering, skim the impurities from the surface of the stock with a ladle to keep the flavour clean and the stock clear. Once the stock has come to a simmer and it has been skimmed, add the tomatoes, parsley and bay leaves, and any mushroom trim that you may have lying around. Continue to simmer the stock for 3 hours, skimming regularly.

Meanwhile, coat the carrots, onions, leek, celery and garlic in a little canola oil and roast them at 180°C for about 45 minutes, turning as required until they are deep golden brown. Once cooked, remove them from the pan and deglaze it as with the chicken bones. Add this liquid and the roast vegetables to the stock.

Cook the stock for a further 1 hour to complete the extraction of flavour from the bones. If at any point the stock drops below the level of the bones, just add more cold water. Once the stock has simmered for around 5 hours, strain it by ladling the stock through a fine sieve twice. Put the strained stock in a smaller saucepan and heat to reduce. Keep simmering the stock and skimming until it reduces by half.

In a separate pot, reduce the Madeira port to about 150 ml and add it to the stock. Once the stock has reduced to about 1 litre it should be at a consistency where it just coats a spoon. Add a couple of sprigs of thyme and some cracked pepper, rest it for half an hour, then strain it for the last time and set it aside.

Caramel jus

MAKES 150–200 ML

500 ml port wine jus
50 ml caramel essence

Bring the port wine jus to the boil and add the caramel essence. Simmer for 10 minutes. It should have a sweet, bitter flavour.

Red wine reduction

MAKES 200–250 ML

2 cups red wine
1 tbsp brown sugar
2 tbsp balsamic vinegar
1 litre venison or beef stock

Place all the ingredients in a pot on the stove and simmer at a low heat for about 45–60 minutes or until the sauce thickens and coats the back of a spoon.

Sweet and sour oranges

2 oranges
¼ cup caster sugar
¼ cup champagne vinegar
½ cup water
zest of 1 lime

Peel the oranges and cut them in half. Place all the other ingredients into a pot and bring to the boil. When the sugar has dissolved, add the oranges and simmer for 5 minutes, then remove the oranges and reduce the liquid to a thick syrup. Pour over the oranges and store.

Orange coulis

MAKES 150 ML

1 x 312 g can mandarin
   segments
200 g orange juice
60 g caster sugar
2 tsp cornflour

Bring the mandarin segments, orange juice and sugar to the boil, then turn down to a simmer. Mix the cornflour with a little water and set aside. Reduce the orange mix by a quarter. Whilst still simmering, add the cornflour a little at a time until the sauce thickens, stirring all the time. Make sure you cook the cornflour out so you get the full required thickness. Using a stick blender or food processor, mix to a thick liquid and put through a strainer to get any lumps out. Set aside to cool and store in the fridge.

Blackcurrant coulis

1 cup blackcurrants
½ cup water
½ cup white sugar

Top and tail the blackcurrants. Combine the blackcurrants, water and sugar and boil in a saucepan for 30 minutes. Press through a sieve to remove the pips and skins. Let cool.

Redcurrant coulis

70 g redcurrant jelly
50 ml red wine
20 ml grenadine
1 tsp cornflour

Place the redcurrant jelly, red wine and grenadine in a heavy-bottomed saucepan and bring to the boil. Cook for 5 minutes, then thicken with cornflour.

Vanilla sugar

1 vanilla pod
sugar

It's nice to always have some vanilla sugar on hand. To make it all you need to do is put a scraped vanilla pod into a container of sugar and you're away. It may take a couple of days for the sugar to take on the fragrance of the vanilla, but once you've got it going you can just keep adding used vanilla pods and sugar as required.

Passion fruit syrup

1 cup caster sugar
100 ml water
100 ml passion fruit juice

Gently warm the sugar and water in a saucepan, then turn the heat up to a simmer and cook to a light-golden syrup. Add the passion fruit juice and reduce to a soft syrup. Allow to cool and serve chilled. This syrup can be stored for up to a month in the fridge.

Raspberry compote

MAKES 750 G

500 g frozen raspberries
250 g caster sugar
50 ml lemon juice

Place all the ingredients in a saucepan and gently heat to dissolve the sugar. Do not stir the raspberries or they will break up. Chill before using.

Hokey pokey

325 g sugar
50 g honey
125 g liquid glucose
100 ml water
20 g baking soda

Gently warm the sugar, honey and glucose in the water, then turn the heat up to a simmer and cook to a light-golden caramel. Sift the baking soda into the caramel and mix well. Be careful as this chemical reaction rises very quickly and is very hot. Pour the mix onto a sheet of baking paper and allow to cool. Break your hokey pokey into bite-size pieces and store them in an airtight container.

Chocolate mousse

MAKES 1.4 KG

3 egg yolks
2 whole eggs
100 g caster sugar
400 g chocolate (72% cocoa solids)
750 ml cream

Use an electric mixer to beat the egg yolks and whole eggs with the sugar until very pale and fluffy. Melt the chocolate in either a double boiler or the microwave. Whip the cream to soft peaks, mix the melted chocolate with the beaten eggs until well combined, then fold into the whipped cream. Chill until set.

And the winners are ...

The Monteith's Beer and Wild Food Challenge began in 1998. For the first few years it was an Auckland-only competition (presumably because cutlery and china plates were yet to reach other parts of the country), with the first winner a wild duck dish created by charismatic chef Jean-Jacques of the Bohemian Café in Ponsonby Road. The trophy stayed in Ponsonby Road the following year, moving along the street to Kamo Restaurant.

The turn of the century saw the competition expand southwards, with restaurants in Wellington and Christchurch showing they too could foot it, or hoof it, with the northerners. Café Névé at Fox Glacier took the West Coast regional title in 2002, and Cook'n with Gas was top in Christchurch and Two Chefs Bistro in Dunedin. Museum Restaurant in Hamilton and Tauranga's Beach St were also regional winners.

In 2004 the competition hotted up as Monteith's Beer and Wild Food Challenge became a national event; suddenly feral animals and vegetables all over the country were fair game for New Zealand's creative culinary minds. That year, perhaps underlining the essence of the Challenge, the Karamea Village Hotel was named national winner, with a main called Bunny Brawn — sliced wild rabbit brawn with Karamea feijoa chutney, served with West Coast greens and matched with Monteith's Golden Ale.

The title stayed in the South Island for 2005, as chef Mark Lane of Dunedin's High Tide Waterfront Restaurant took the top honour — a natural progression perhaps, as Mark had won the regional title two years previously. Hamilton restaurant Canvas also gained a lot of attention that year, by putting horse on the menu. Mr Ed Is Dead might have upset a few, but hundreds more galloped in for a taste.

Christchurch's Alchemy Restaurant won the formal category in 2006, with head chef Glenn Andrews' Bunny in a Basket (matched with Monteith's Original). Hamilton's Embargo won the informal category.

In 2007 Stephen Barry, of Mount Bistro in Mount Maunganui, came up with Sword 'n' Sauce-ry — a skewer of scallops, prawn tail, crayfish, salmon and fresh fish flambéed with horopito and lime vodka — to take line honours.

Wellington's The General Practitioner came in first in 2008. Head chef Andy Potts developed two wild dishes, with stinging nettle in one followed by a seafood arrangement in the other, which wowed the judges and knocked out the ten other regional winners.

Auckland triumphed in 2009. The Abbey Bar and Kitchen in Greenlane had another award on the wall after Eugene Sokolovski devised a lavender-crusted venison rack with a taro and green banana-filled apple, redcurrants, goat cheese and golden kumara soufflé, and maple-poached Jerusalem artichokes.

The Porch Kitchen and Bar of Waihi was crowned winner in 2010, as chef Brad King fought off six other finalist chefs from around the country with his wild pork-themed Boarack Meets Underbelly, matched with Monteith's Pilsner. That year, Linda Hammond from Bulls won the inaugural Monteith's Wild Food Recipe Competition with her smoky eel, mussel and gurnard risotto, matched with Monteith's Golden Lager.

And, in 2011, Taupo's Plateau Restaurant and Bar emerged victorious as head chef Jude Messenger's Four Wild Pigs in the Orchard, matched with Monteith's Crushed Apple Cider, outdid over 100 restaurants throughout New Zealand.

Acknowledgements

I would like to thank Andre Taber and Kristeen Yelavich, who put in hours of work establishing first contact with the chefs who contributed recipes for this book.

I would also like to acknowledge those chefs who took up our challenge and freely contributed recipes, often making a major effort to present them in such a way so that they are accessible to the home cook.

Acknowledgement must go also to journalist Doug Coutts, who assisted with bringing together the legends and anecdotes about Monteith's Brewing Co. and the characters who made it the great company we recognize today.

Thanks to photographer Devin Hart. Young, talented, responsive and the perfect gentleman, he made our job easier than it might have been.

At Monteith's, thank you to Jennie Macindoe, Marketing Manager, for sourcing historical images, Monteith's branding and the history of Monteith's.

The most significant thanks must go to chef Alan Brown, who unwittingly took on the task of preparing the dishes ready for photography. It proved to be an enormous and complex job that required an amount of work that went way beyond the scope of our initial brief. Yet not once during the long and involved process did his energy abate or his enthusiasm fade. He is a bona fide Masterchef who takes enormous pride in his work and brings to every occasion consummate skill and professionalism.

Alan would like to thank Olaf's Artisan Bakery and Café for supplying breads; Great Taste New Zealand for horopito, kawakawa, harakeke, pikopiko and game meats; Premium Game for game meats; Innes Moffat, Venison Marketing Servicing Manager at Deer Industry New Zealand, for farmed venison; and Christine McDonald, Purchasing Manager at AUT School of Hospitality and Tourism, who was a great help in sourcing and purchasing ingredients.

A note from the author

The recipes in this book came to us in a variety of forms and levels of complexity. For the sake of consistency we were required to make some changes, substitute more common ingredients for those unavailable to the home cook, and revise some quantities to make them work outside the restaurant environment. In addition, we were required to assemble each dish in a way that showed off as many of the elements as we could, and yet preserve their integrity for photography. As a result, many dishes are styled very differently from the way they may be styled by the chef who created them. We intend no slight whatsoever to the contributing chef, and trust that the way the dishes are illustrated serves only to encourage readers to don their aprons, fire up their stoves and get cooking — because no matter how we made the dishes appear, they are all very, very good and totally worthy of being attempted by all readers.

Stockists

Deer Industry New Zealand www.deernz.co.nz
Great Taste New Zealand www.greattastenz.co.nz
Harmony Foods www.harmony.co.nz
Neat Meat www.neatmeat.co.nz
Olaf's Artisan Bakery and Café www.olafs.co.nz
Premium Game www.game-meats.co.nz
Raukumara Red www.wildvenison.co.nz
Razorback New Zealand www.wildboar.co.nz

Contributors

Alabaster, Liz, Monteith's Brewery Bar, Alexandra
Ball, Daniel, No. 4, Christchurch
Barry, Denny, The Quarry Tavern, Te Puna
Barry, Stephen, Mount Bistro, Mount Maunganui
Beehre, Kristopher, Ambrosia Restaurant and Bar, Rotorua
Bhaskaran, Robbie, 1841 Bar and Restaurant, Wellington
Cahill, Michelle, Dickens Inn, Whangarei
Carr, Michael, House on Hood, Hamilton
Chittock, Sharron, Monty's Bar and Restaurant, Queenstown
Clarke, Andrew, Victoria Street Bistro, Hamilton
Comerso, Emiliano Sebastian, St Moritz, Queenstown
Corbett, Scott, Pepper Tree Restaurant and Bar, Coromandel
Cutler, Colin, The Coalface, Greymouth
Dallow, Luke, Chapel Bar and Bistro, Auckland
Dorquiraj, Dwayne, The Zookeeper's Son, Auckland
Farley, Matthew, Piko at AUT University, Auckland
Finlayson, John, The Watershed, Christchurch
Hayward-Swain, Andrew, Heartland Hotel, Gore
Hogg, Cody, Phil's Place, Tauranga
Jerkovich, Scott, Fort Street Union, Auckland
Katipa, Shannon, The White Swan, Greytown
Kelly, Steve, The Brewer's Apprentice, Palmerston North
Kornkaset, Jessada, The Thirsty Marriner, Christchurch
Lobao, Sandro, New Orleans Hotel, Arrowtown
Lumsden, Timothy, The Porch Kitchen and Bar, Waihi
McMillan, Hayden, TriBeCa Restaurant and Bar, Auckland
Messenger, Jude, Plateau Restaurant and Bar, Taupo
Miller, Greg, The Thirsty Whale, Napier
Miller, Peter, The Riverhead, Auckland
Mold, John, Monteith's Brewery Bar, Wellington
Redward, Louisa, Ploughmans, Taupo
Scott, Geoff, Vinnies Restaurant, Auckland
Seidel, Jenny, Redoubt Bar and Eatery, Matamata
Sokolovski, Eugene, Ribier Restaurant, Auckland
Southon, Mark, The Foodstore, Auckland
Stella, Diego, The Drake, Auckland
Tyack, Kerry, Auckland
Wigglesworth, Megan, Villager, Auckland
Wiperi, Tom, Smith and McKenzie Chophouse, Hamilton

Index